How to
SURVIVE
Your Husband's
Midlife Crisis

Strategies and Stories from THE MIDLIFE WIVES CLUB

Gay Courter and Pat Gaudette

A Perigee Book

A Perigee Book
Published by The Berkley Publishing Group
A division of Penguin Group (USA) Inc.
375 Hudson Street
New York, New York 10014

First edition: May 2003

Library of Congress Cataloging-in-Publication Data

Gaudette, Pat.
How to survive your husband's midlife crisis : strategies and stories from the Midlife Wives Club / Pat Gaudette and Gay Courter.—1st ed.
p.cm.
Includes bibliographical references and index.
ISBN 0-399-52882-2
1. Middle aged men—Psychology. 2. Husbands—Psychology. 3. Midlife crisis. 4. Middle aged women—Psychology. 5. Wives—Psychology. I. Courter, Gay. II. Midlife club. III. Title.

HQ1059.4.G38 2003
155.6'5—dc21   2003043326

Printed in the United States of America

10 9 8 7 6 5 4 3 2 1

How to
SURVIVE
Your Husband's
Midlife Crisis

Strategies and Stories from THE MIDLIFE WIVES CLUB

Also by Gay Courter

THE BEANSPROUT BOOK

THE MIDWIFE

RIVER OF DREAMS

CODE EZRA

FLOWERS IN THE BLOOD

THE MIDWIFE'S ADVICE

I SPEAK FOR THIS CHILD: TRUE STORIES OF A CHILD ADVOCATE

*Dedicated to
the past and present members of the Midlife Wives Club,
who generously shared their stories to help others
through their perilous journeys.*

*For future members:
Welcome to the sisterhood of survivors!*

Love is the whole history of a woman's life,
it is but an episode in a man's.

—Madame de Staël, written in 1796, age 30

CONTENTS

Welcome to the Club

We are never so defenseless against suffering as when we love, never so helplessly unhappy as when we have lost our love object or its love.

—Sigmund Freud, written in 1930, age 74

You are in a committed relationship, married or involved exclusively with one another. You thought everything was glorious—or, at least as glorious as it gets. All relationships have some rough spots. But now it seems that you are always fighting. Or he just doesn't act like himself anymore. He doesn't like his job. He wants a sportier car. He says you and he have grown apart. He wants something but he doesn't know what.

All relationships have their difficult times, but when a previously sensible man morphs into an angry stranger, the difficulties compound. Does your man say he is no longer "in love" with you but his reasons, if any, are vague at best? Is he trying to reinvent himself as a younger, hipper guy? Is he looking for an elusive "something" that he can't define? Have you twisted yourself inside out in an attempt to please him, but with no success? Maybe it's time you stop trying to change yourself and focus on the real cause of his conduct. If this is new behavior for him and he is between the ages of 35 and 50, your man is blazing a trail through midlife—and he is probably having a crisis. But how do you know for sure? And if it *is* a crisis, what can you do about it?

You are not alone. Pat Gaudette has been through a midlife crisis twice—first as the person in crisis, then as the person affected by the crisis—and wanted to help others find their way through this confusing time. Because she understood the importance of having a strong support system, she established the Midlife Wives Club on the Internet for women caught in the middle of their man's crisis, and later went on to write this book.

To join the Midlife Wives Club, log on to *www.midlife wivesclub.com*. Here you will find women sharing their experiences, giving advice to others, and finding answers to the questions that had been undermining their confidence. In this safe place, you will discover not only a sisterhood of survivors, but also a surprising bonus: men—themselves bewildered by their jumbled feelings—who provide another viewpoint that may help fit the puzzle together. Women's midlife crises are also explored online. However, this book is a window into *male* midlife crisis primarily from the perspective of the women who take this unexpected journey—even though they were not planning to go and their bags were not packed.

When you read the stories on the website, you will not find the contributors' names as they appear in this book (with the exception of the authors Pat Gaudette and Gay Courter). Most participants select screen names. While screen identities work in an online environment, Midlife Wives Club members are real people telling intimate stories, so we decided to give them fictional first names. We told online club members a book was in progress. Some chose to actively participate in the process, filled out questionnaires, picked pseudonyms for themselves and their partners, and altered other aspects of their identity. We assigned other contributors fictitious names.

Midlife Wives Club members log on worldwide, but while a region or country may be specified, no location is precise. The Internet is a global community, and midlife issues are faced by most couples to some degree—whether they live in Australia or Alabama, Japan or Johannesburg, London or Louisville. One of the strengths of the club is the support network that is available 24/7, regardless of time zone, because when people are distraught, they need immediate assistance and comfort.

While a few of the members' posts contain direct quotes, all have been edited for conciseness and clarity, as well as fictionalized further to protect anonymity. Pat, who pioneered the website, is sharing the story of her second marriage with "Frank"; however that husband's name has been changed. She is married again and nothing in this book reflects any aspect of that marriage. Gay has been married to Philip (real name) for 35 years. Nobody, except for Pat herself and Gay's family, is identified correctly. If someone sees their real name or that of a spouse, it is merely a coincidence.

How to Survive Your Husband's Midlife Crisis contains the wisdom distilled from hundreds of thousands of anguished queries from apprehensive women and empathetic responses from the seasoned veterans who share their survival tactics. The contributors are mostly Americans, but there is strong international representation. Most are the partners of middle-aged men or are having relationship issues and find many of the discussions on subjects like marital disputes, adultery, abuse, abandonment, and divorce are pertinent to them. Some of the women are relieved to learn that their worst fears are not justified. Others see the pieces of their marital puzzle lining up to form the picture of a classic crisis. *How to Survive Your Hus-*

band's Midlife Crisis will show how other wives began to suspect something was wrong. Some found out in one rude awakening. For others the realization came more slowly. For every woman the news is shattering, and she must face an onslaught of decisions and choices as she ventures on her unanticipated expedition. All along the way, fellow travelers down this bumpy road will share their experiences as well as their varied perspectives. Some women may choose to leave their spouses, others stand by their men through thick or thin. Many feel they have been left with no choices when their mates leave them. When the men chime in, their point of view is set off in "His Turn" sections, because understanding the nature of the beast is crucial before making life-changing decisions.

What are the men feeling? Is this a typical rite of passage? Will he get over it? Will life return to "normal"? Is every man vulnerable? Is he depressed, and might therapy or medication help? *How to Survive Your Husband's Midlife Crisis* includes the latest research—and controversies—on male midlife crisis. Social scientists disagree about how to define this phenomenon and whether there is a male counterpart to a woman's menopause. But just as every 2-year-old learns the word "no!" and most teenagers turn ornery, every person experiences a midlife turning point to some degree. Around the time Pat's second husband, Frank, became a grandfather, a serious illness forced him to face his own mortality, and the weak economy pushed their business to the brink of bankruptcy. The cumulative stress resulted in a midlife crisis. While Gay's husband, Philip, did not have to confront so many issues simultaneously, he was not immune to the doubts that come when a man realizes half his life is over. Pat's husband bought motorcycles and sailboats. Gay's lusted after a classic sports car but ended up with an airplane. Pat and Frank drifted apart and agreed to a divorce. A plane crash helped Gay and Philip clarify their goals and values, and they adopted an older child from foster care. Pat found contentment in a new career and subsequent marriage. Not every couple will identify their transitions as a crisis, but they probably have experienced alterations, choices, and changes from mild discontent to full-blown upheaval. Some couples are adept in traversing the obstacle course of life as a team, others have a harder time working together or overcoming individual problems from their past that cannot be repressed at midlife. Long-time club members show how the midlife crisis experience evolves. Some of the participants who have been members of the club for many years share the long-term progress of their crisis. In Chapter 10 we learn how their crises resolved and the current status of their marriages.

The Midlife Wives Club is an interactive website with a forum, which is arranged by current discussion topics, that offers immediate feedback to questions and a way to express feelings and get help. *How to Survive Your Husband's Midlife Crisis* has distilled the best material and advice from thousands of postings on topics like how to tell your children and family, what to do if you suspect infidelity, and how to deal with your emotional rollercoaster. Worried mates will find practical advice on everything from what to do today to planning your future with—or without—the man who seems to be changing before your eyes. We urge readers to join the club online to get answers to their own questions and also to use the resources in the book's appendix to locate other pertinent websites and books that club members report helped them cope.

CHAPTER 1

The Unexpected Journey: When a Marriage Changes—and Why

All happy families are like one another;
each unhappy family is unhappy in its own way.

—Leo Tolstoy, written in 1877, age 49

Did Tolstoy, in his opening line of *Anna Karenina*, get it right? Or when men stray and marriages fray, are there also patterns that can help those whose lives are torn apart make sense out of the commotion? The novel's next two sentences point out that "Everything was in confusion in the Oblonsky household. The wife had found out that the husband had had an affair with their French governess and had told him that she could not go on living in the same house with him." In nineteenth-century Russia Oblonsky sent for his sister, Anna, to help Dolly Oblonsky accept her husband's infidelity as dalliance of no consequence. But when Anna had a tempestuous affair of her own, her act brought shame, ruin, the loss of her children, and the eventual tragic ending.

Twenty-first-century women who find their marriages crumbling are not as legally or socially dependent on their husbands and so, thankfully, have more options. But the double standard still exists—contemporary women have been proselytized by a Judeo-Christian ethic that prescribes fidelity, while some anthropologists and sociologists point out that monogamy is not the natural state for the human male and that other cultures accept a man's need for variety. Media aimed at women promotes soulmates and happily ever after, while the publicity blitz that targets men is adorned with nubile babes. So is it any wonder that Marilyn Monroe turned on her neighbor's *Seven Year Itch* or that Dudley Moore found Bo Derek irresistible in *10*?

When the romance begins to wither and there are more clashes than kisses, worried wives turn to their computers and go online in search for answers. In this circle of compassion and support, they pour out their hearts to anonymous listeners and find a large set of cyber-shoulders on which to lean. These are mostly women who are in varying stages of dealing with men who have taken the proverbial midlife hike. Some of their mates are showing the early signs of insecurity and dissatisfaction with many aspects of their humdrum lives, leaving them and their children in the dust of their newfound freedom. These women learn that they have become reluctant members of a club, whose seasoned members know where they are coming from as well as where they might be heading. For, just like some other of life's major turning points, such as falling in love, getting married, giving birth, facing serious illness, and experiencing death, a spouse's midlife crisis has predictable stages and patterns. These patterns are sometimes hard to recognize when you are lost in the private forest of churning emotions, but they are obvious to those who have already passed through them.

Rude Awakenings: First Signs of Trouble

Many members of the Midlife Wives Club recall with excruciating accuracy the precise moment they knew their lives would never be the same. Grace had a premonition. Her husband, Roger, had returned to England from a trip overseas. After sleeping late, he said he wanted to take a walk to get some fresh air and buy a paper. Grace was anxious to hear about his trip and watched the clock. He seemed to be taking much longer than expected. She began to pace the house, which was tidy and clean. She had stayed up into the early hours making everything perfect for him, because before the trip, he complained about the children's messes and how he yearned for "clean spaces." "The fact that I was trying so hard to please him while he was planning to leave me chokes me to this day."

Then, she saw his briefcase by the front door, where the children's backpacks usually littered the hallway. She picked it up to keep the area neat, but for some reason, she popped open the clasp and noticed a packet of condoms. "My heart was thudding, but I felt incredibly calm," Grace said, "even though I knew from that moment my life would never be the same again."

But it hadn't been a bolt out of the blue. Grace had known for a long time Roger was unhappy with his life. He had become depressed the previous year and was taking antidepressants. He was losing his hair, which bothered him. Plus he lost his parents within a short duration of each other and felt guilty that he hadn't spent more time with them in recent years. He felt pressure at work and at home, and he looked forward to the business trip because he said it might help give him some "needed space."

As Grace walked slowly down the street to meet him, she

noticed a guarded look in his eyes. She spoke in the calmest voice she could muster. "Do you have anything to tell me?" He said no and she repeated the question. Roger appeared flustered and shook his head. "Are you having an affair?" Grace asked.

Again Roger denied it, but Grace asked once more. This time he admitted it. "I felt as if I had been punched in the stomach," she said, "yet I couldn't stop asking the questions that would hurt me more: how long it had been going on, how old she was—twenty years younger than me!—and if he was still seeing her. Roger told me the affair started six months earlier and reminded me of the day he called in a panic when he learned there had been a takeover bid for his company and they were talking about who might be redundant. I remember thinking that was such a harsh word for someone who had given ten years to his job, and how my heart had gone out to him. He said he had to work late, which I understood, but instead he went out with her. I kept up the interrogation until he confessed that he loved her. From that moment, my marriage of 18 years was over."

Another woman, Annie*, could barely bring herself to recall the moment she faced the truth. It was especially painful for her because as a reporter in Nashville, she was used to uncovering other people's dirty secrets, but chose to ignore her husband Larry's unexplained absences. One day, on a whim, she opened the accounting files. "He paid the bills and dealt with the taxes—chores I hated—so he hadn't hidden the receipts for jewelry and lingerie. But there they were: the proof my marriage was a lie. Up until then, I had a starry-eyed naiveté about love that made my heart turn over every time I saw Larry walk in the

*Find out the current status of Annie's relationship in Chapter 10. Other members whose names are marked with an asterisk at first mention are also updated in Chapter 10.

door. To think I felt that way even though he had been with another woman!"

Like Annie, Lee* avoided all the signs. "I had been out of town for my father-in-law's funeral and stayed a few extra days to help my mother-in-law. The children went home to Wisconsin with my husband. A neighbor agreed to take care of the children after school until their father got home from work. They were at her house when I got back in town, so I went over to pick them up." Lee wanted to hurry home to unpack, but the neighbor asked her to come into the kitchen for a cup of coffee.

" 'There's something I have to tell you about,' she said, then told me how she had seen James with another woman at a local park. I was about to say it could have been someone from work and she shouldn't jump to conclusions when she said they were kissing. I looked straight at her and said, 'Not my James, he wouldn't do that, there is no way he would ever do anything like that!' I asked if she could feed the kids supper, then went home and confronted James when he walked in the door." James began to cry and begged Lee to believe he had needed to talk to someone who'd experienced the loss of a father. Lee asked him about the kiss, and he swore the neighbor had been exaggerating a friendly peck on the cheek. Still Lee suspected there was more to it.

All these women were blindsided by revelations that their marriages were far rockier than they had imagined. Why? Was it something they had done? Had their spouses been tempted by another woman? Had their husbands changed over time, and they had failed to notice the signs?

Slow Dawning Realizations:
Putting the Clues Together

For Colleen* there was no lightning strike that fractured her life into "before" and "after." Like many club members, her problems began with loving concern. Why was her husband, Rory, behaving so oddly? "At first I suspected he was heading toward a depression, due to the culture shock of our move to Japan. He had many signs of depression—being constantly irritated, drinking more than a few cocktails every evening, and experiencing job dissatisfaction. What worried me most was the lack of sexual interest, because we used to make love three or four times a week. I knew he was unhappy with his job, but his level of anger seemed out of proportion to the situation. Then he started criticizing everything I did."

One day, when Colleen was washing the dishes, she broke a cheap wineglass and cut her finger slightly. Instead of asking her if she was okay, Rory growled, "You would have to break my favorite one, wouldn't you?"

"I clutched my bleeding finger and sobbed, not because it hurt but because I felt as if I couldn't do anything right. This made Rory even more annoyed and he asked, 'What the hell is wrong with you these days?' "

All of a sudden Colleen knew it was not about her and voiced the question she had never dared ask: "Do you still want me in your life or not?"

"I'm not sure," he answered in his professorial voice as though it was a response to an academic inquiry. She asked if there was another woman. "He claimed he hadn't had an affair (but he had), and there was no one else in his life (but there was). And since I wasn't ready to accept the situation, I believed him."

Still, the seeds of distrust had been sown, and soon bits and pieces that should have previously set off little bells finally triggered an all-out alarm. Six weeks later, Colleen not only figured out there was someone else in Rory's life, but who she was. "One of his students had gone abroad for an extended research trip, and the reason Rory was depressed was that he missed her terribly. I had seen the postcards and knew he had been corresponding with this student by e-mail, but there were far too many communications for a casual student-teacher relationship." Colleen became even more infuriated when she recalled that Rory had asked that his lonely student be invited to Christmas dinner at their home. "Even so, I did not catch on for the longest time," Colleen said, incredulous at her own level of denial.

In Australia, Evie*, who worked with her husband, Robert, says she first suspected something was wrong when he suddenly started referring to her as his "partner" instead of his wife. When she first mentioned the change, he said he thought clients would respect her work more than if she was just the "wife." That made sense, but there were other worrisome changes. "Robert withdrew from many of his normal activities, resigned from community committees, stopped going to his beloved car club, and although he used to enjoy being a Mr. Fix-it, wouldn't lift a finger around the house." He was also rude to old friends and their social life suffered. Robert became exasperated by the noise the children made and anything she did wrong.

"Instead of going to sleep with me, as he had done throughout our marriage, he would steal away to his computer, stay up till all hours, and then sleep late in the morning. One night I tried to get him to come to bed with me to make love," Evie said, "and he refused by saying that if he didn't want it, he couldn't do it. That was the moment I finally accepted our marriage was in trouble."

Joining the Club: Finding Support Online

The casual observer might characterize these men as typical guys trying to bust out of a stagnant marriage or looking to have an affair on the side. Yet each situation was triggered by an underlying midlife crisis. In the United States alone, there are more than 29 million American males between the ages of 40 and 55 who are going through what author Jed Diamond refers to as the "male menopause passage." Of course only a small fraction of these men's marriages are wrecked by their reaction to the emotional and physical changes brought on by the natural aging process called andropause. Less well documented than female menopause, the biochemical changes that men do experience create a complex syndrome with a wide range of reactions. Some of these mimic depression and may be more acute if there are additional stresses in their lives such as the death of a parent, job pressures, or tension at home.

Just as falling in love can either happen at first sight or grow more gradually, falling apart has its variations. Whether the news of a change comes as a complete shock or in a more complex equation over time, the results for women involved with men experiencing a midlife crisis are the same. They find themselves alone, adrift, saddened, terrified, and with numerous unanswered questions. Pat wished there had been some place to turn when her second husband's behavior changed. It was the later realization that her situation hadn't been unique that caused her to focus her publishing skills on developing relationship-oriented publications, beginning with a magazine for mature singles called *Friends & Lovers: The Magazine for Singles over 40*. Then, in 1996, Pat went online to create a web version of her publication. As Pat read the posts to the midlife crisis section of her relationships forum, she realized these contributors needed a place to discuss this precise issue. Thus she founded the midlife crisis support site, the Midlife Wives Club (*www.midlifewivesclub.com*).

Originally established for women, the Midlife Wives Club now provides support to both men and women, giving each valuable insights into the other side of midlife issues. The most popular part of the site is the forum, where readers go to meet and share ideas and experiences. There you can read messages from others, ask questions, interact, and exchange concerns with other members.

After someone suggested Colleen's husband's peculiar behavior might be a form of midlife crisis, she typed the words into a search engine. Pat's introductory essay, "His Midlife Crisis!," popped up, and it struck a chord with her. Colleen showed it to her husband, but he brushed it off. The day after Colleen confronted Rory about his other woman, she started asking questions online. "It was the best thing I could have done," she said. "At last I had some answers."

Pain is a lonely experience and hard to describe. Those who have felt a similar anguish know what to say to soothe and support. Advice is more easily accepted from someone who has walked in your boots—and made it through the blizzard—than a professional giving theoretical advice about how to prepare for a bitter climate. Pat's counsel was born from experience, and her website soon became a haven for thousands of others who needed to fasten their seat belts in preparation for the bumpiest ride of their lives.

Cries for Help: Logging On for Cyber Support

"Last night my husband told me that he wasn't happy, didn't know why, and that it had been coming on for a long time. He doesn't know if it is me or not," Alice wrote in her first post to the Midlife Wives Club. "He talked about a divorce, or maybe a separation, but isn't sure what he wants. I am in shock. I didn't have a clue that this is what Tyrone was thinking. We do everything together—go to ballgames, parties, and work on our rental property. When I come home from work, he's waiting for me to go running with him. Then boom, he drops the bomb. He's moving into an apartment for a while. He never asked how I felt about all this or gave me any options. What do I do now? Help me please!"

"Alice, sorry this happened to you," responded Katie. "Even though none of us chose to be here, you will find hope, comfort, warmth, experience, and more from some of the nicest people you will probably ever 'meet.' Think of this as a first aid station. As you work your way through our messages, you will see some of us are starting out like you, some are smack-dab in the middle, and others are coming to the conclusion of their own journey. Each of us has a unique story to tell, yet you will be amazed at the similarities. (Sometimes we wonder if we are all married to the same man!) Even though this appears to have come out of the blue (and given you a major case of the blues), didn't you have any inkling that something had changed?"

"This is what I keep asking myself," Alice typed back. "Tyrone is 38, self-employed, very stressed. He hadn't been sleeping well, he was easily irritated, and he worked longer hours, but I saw no change toward me. We continued to sleep together—in both senses of the word—but he became more moody. He'd say, 'I think I'm losing my mind' and 'This house is driving me crazy' and 'My mind won't quit thinking.' I told him he'd get through this and I loved him."

Jasmine piped in, "*You* didn't do anything wrong. This is *his* problem, *his* trip. But we'll be here to help you figure out what is going on."

Almost daily someone like Alice discovers the website, and while their questions are familiar to long-term members, there is always a friendly welcome. As Tish* told one distraught first-time poster, "It's only been one week. Your world has collapsed. You have to feel all these emotions and you can't skip any of them. Have you ever had to grieve a death or deal with a severe illness for you or a loved one? This is a similar process of sadness and disbelief."

For newcomers, who are shell-shocked by the changes in their relationship, Annie answers the most frequently asked questions. "To our new friends here: Nothing is ever a hundred percent your fault. You are finding yourself in a heartbreaking situation, a place you never thought you would be. You are hurt, angry, humiliated, and confused. You do not understand why this happened, and you, naturally, blame yourself. Please do not. There are countless reasons for a rough time in a relationship.

"Right now you cannot think clearly because that heavy stone you are carrying in your chest gets in the way of everything else," Annie explains. "Talk about how you feel to us here, but also seek help from someone you can trust, whether it is a family member, a pastor, or a counselor. However, do not reveal your private problems to too many people, and that includes family members. If or when the issues are resolved and you are reunited with your spouse, friends or family members who were supportive when you were hurting so badly may voice reservations about him. So be selective. The lessons you learn will bring you strength, courage, a new independence, and confidence that will sustain you no matter the outcome of the relationship."

Peer support groups have become an accepted way to treat stressful situations. Many people find that self-help groups are an invaluable resource for recovery and empowerment. Just like groups in which people meet in person to deal with life-disrupting events such as death, abuse, addiction, divorce, or the diagnosis of a physical or mental disability, the Midlife Wives Club offers a place where people share information with others going through various stages of the same problem or those who have survived. Participation online is voluntary and anonymous, making it easier to share confidential information. A woman experiencing the full-frontal attack of her husband's midlife crisis may feel that it is a life-threatening experience. Indeed it does endanger her way of life up until that time.

Just like a serious medical diagnosis may stimulate feelings of isolation, despondency, and helplessness, so may the realization that a man's midlife issues are eating away at a marriage. And just as psychosocial groups for patients with cancer have been able to improve patients' quality of life, with beneficial effects on coping, distress level, anxiety, depression, and pain, so does participation in an online support group. Even more remarkable, according to a study reported in *Lancet*, women with metastatic breast cancer who participated in a year-long support group survived significantly longer (36.6 versus 18.9 months) than those who did not.

After a dreadful year dealing with Lance's crisis, Dottie wrote, "Getting support from other club members just as the garbage hit the fan helped me immensely. Seeing how others picked their way through the minefield helped me make better choices."

In the newcomer's section, Chloe provides a few pointers for new arrivals:

- Never let him see you cry.

- Never beg him for anything.

- Let him believe you are doing fine.

- Don't tell him to leave the house unless you want him to go.

- Don't ask him questions about anything if you might not be ready to hear his answer.

- Don't try to involve him in deep discussions about your relationship.

- Take care of yourself and treat yourself with respect.

- Be true to yourself.

The Walking Wounded: Reacting to the Chaos of Your Mate's Midlife Crisis

When a woman experiences a sudden change from a stable state to an unbalanced one, her world seems to tilt. Every step is an uphill climb. Every breath is harder to take. Emotions are difficult to control, and they may vacillate between rage and despair, sorrow and resentment. Bottled-up feelings find release in crying or shouting. Some women internalize the pain and become ill; others take it out on co-workers, family, and children.

"For the first few days I cried so much that I have no idea how the human body can produce so many tears," Evie said after her husband returned from an overseas trip and moved in with the woman with whom he had been traveling. "I wanted to hide in a hole. I did have to take care of the kids so that was what got me out of bed. The slightest memories would set me off. I couldn't listen to the radio because songs we had sung together in the car made me wonder if he was singing them with her."

Bonnie was upset because she had to leave her once-familiar surroundings. "I thought it was only going to be a brief separation and I couldn't afford the mortgage, so I moved out. I left most of my possessions behind, but at least I took the computer.

Somehow I knew I would need it for more than playing solitaire." The couples counselor they had seen mentioned something about midlife crisis, so she typed the words into the Ask Jeeves search engine and found the Midlife Wives Club. "Then I spent the first month crying, barely holding on to my new job, and talking with friends long distance and online."

Megan* laughed when she recalled her first reaction to her husband's plans to take the proverbial hike—alone. "In movies nobody ever shows the part after someone throws the wineglass. Well, the rest of the story is that someone has to sweep up the shards of crystal and wipe the sherry off the walls. Who do you think had to do that?" Megan's tone became more serious. "After that, I realized how alone I was and I broke into uncontrollable sobs. Through my tears I dialed the phone and poured out my story to anyone who would listen. Your real friends are the ones who'll talk to you in the middle of the night." Megan also stopped sleeping and began smoking again. "Since I am self-employed as a computer programmer, I put in as many hours as I could without falling over and I also worked my way through the wine cellar. I think I would have gone crazy if I hadn't found this support group."

"I cannot remember the first month after he left," Katie chimed in. "It is all a blur. I think I went crazy."

"Me too," agreed Tish. "It is painful even to remember how I spent the first day not only crying but rolled up in a ball on the floor. I was in so much agony I felt like I needed to go to the emergency room. I told a friend I literally thought I was going to die of a broken heart. She convinced me to see my doctor the next day, which turned out to be the right thing to do."

Kelly was desperate when she logged on. "I am in so much pain I am not sure I can go on past the next minute. I am not suicidal, just in pain. I always thought heartache was only a saying, but this is much worse, like I've been stabbed in the chest.

He told me he has finally decided he is leaving on Tuesday and wants me to explain it to the kids. How can I do that when I can't even explain it to myself?"

Jenelle offered Kelly sage advice. "His eyes are focused on the door right now, so there is nothing you can do to make him stay. Try to center and calm yourself. You will get through this horrible day and things will get better. We'll be here for you."

Finding Local Support

While cyberhugs create a sisterhood of shared feelings, newcomers often need local support to survive the first hours and days as they adjust to a new reality. "If the roof on your home seems to be blowing off, you need to find immediate shelter for yourself and your children," Elinor suggested. "While therapists, attorneys, and other professionals may end up in your life eventually, you need first aid to get through the first days and weeks. Let a few trusted friends know part of your predicament. Merely having someone invite you to dinner or pick up the kids from school may relieve you of one less hassle. Clergy are all too familiar with midlife crisis so don't hesitate to ask for pastoral help, even if you haven't been a regular worshiper."

For Tish, the hardest part was getting out of bed and tending to daily chores. "But I knew I had to get to work to pay the bills and that turned out to be a welcome respite from my empty house. Since I would get calls from Marv that reduced me to tears, I had to clue in my co-workers, and they were understanding." One of them encouraged her to call her doctor. "He started me on anti-anxiety and antidepressant medications, which took the edge off." For a few weeks Tish avoided close friends and family, but admitted this was a mistake. "A friend convinced me to come for a quick cup of coffee, and I felt much better being around someone familiar who was sympathetic to my woes. Soon I was accepting all invitations to be with friends."

Tish loved to read for pleasure, but she couldn't concentrate, although she gobbled up anything she could find about midlife crisis. She also found solace caring for her dogs and soon realized that hiking with them was a way to burn off the tension that gripped her. Renting videos that made her laugh was another stress reliever. "Going online and participating in the Midlife Wives Club was the turning point for me," Tish explained, "but I think I got more out of giving support to others than merely taking it."

Taking Care of Number One

There are three responses to crisis: coping, creating, and transforming. If someone feels she is in a crisis, she is! But that does not mean she doesn't have to continue functioning. Some of the simplest activities like eating, sleeping, working, talking to people, paying the bills, and caring for children may seem as difficult as climbing a mountain. But as the lingo goes, "You still gotta deal." The first step is to develop a coping strategy.

Lee advises the initiates, "Wisdom comes through experiencing something yourself so be prepared to stretch in directions you may have never thought possible. Believe in yourself and your self-worth. Keep your dignity and faith strong. Don't make changes or drastic decisions that you may regret later, but when push comes to shove, save yourself before saving your marriage."

Midlife Wives Club members offer the following suggestions to manage the first difficult days and weeks:

- Enlist helpers (wise friends, close relatives).

- Hire a "professional relative" such as a therapist.

- See a pastoral counselor.

- Consult your doctor for medication to help you sleep, if necessary.

- Avoid self-medicating with alcohol, or illegal or prescription drugs.

- Eat nutritiously, but occasionally indulge yourself in "comfort food."

- Eat smaller meals more frequently—your stomach may feel tied in knots.

- Try crunchy foods, especially fresh ones like carrots, celery, apples—they help dissipate tension and anger.

- Keep your fluids up, but avoid excess caffeine and stimulants.

- Don't start smoking, especially if you once quit, or increase your intake of nicotine.

- Keep up routines (mealtimes, bedtimes, weekly cycles) as much as possible.

- Exercise, including taking long walks, bicycling, or working out on machines, to burn off anger.

- Play music that pleases and soothes you.

- Dress in clothes you like and make you appear your best, regardless of how you may actually feel.

- Treat yourself to long, warm baths, rich desserts, favorite movies, flowers, candles with pleasing scents.

- Read books for escape as well as pragmatic advice.

- Renew friendships you may have neglected.

- Do something creative with your rage: Paint a picture, work with clay, build a shop project, paint a room, write a poem, keep a diary, plant a garden, or weed an overgrown patch.

- Don't forget humor! Tune into sit-coms, rent funny videos, or learn jokes to tell your kids.

- Take pleasure in a passing butterfly, a blossom, a child's first step, a teen's giggling phone conversation, a friend's success.

- Think about someone else. Share a meal with an elderly neighbor. Call a friend who has struggled through a life-threatening illness, even if it wasn't recent. This may not be the best time to add any burdens to your life by volunteering or accepting new commitments, but there are people far worse off, and some people say it helped them to help others.

- Pray or meditate. Welcome the spirituality that might nurture you.

- Imagine how you would like your life to be in the near and far future.

Women who look back on the first days and months of crisis with the wisdom of hindsight know that "this too will pass." As difficult as it may seem during the darkest hours, women must hold on to the dreams they have for a brighter future, although the future may not be the one envisioned before everything changed. If a woman understands what is happening, she may be able to recover much of what was lost. By following the roadmap offered by other survivors, women will be able to take the steps to first figure out what they really want—and then get what they need and deserve.

CHAPTER 2

The Call of the Road: Male Midlife Panic

Do not go gentle into that good night,
Old age should burn and rave at close of day;
Rage, rage against the dying of the light.

—Dylan Thomas, written in 1952, age 38

"There was one moment when I think Frank went from 'stud' to 'geezer'—at least in his own mind," Pat recalled. "He opened a package from his daughter and pulled out a T-shirt with little handprints and the word 'Gramps' underneath in childish scrawl. Before he got that T-shirt, I don't think the reality of being old enough to be a grandfather had ever hit him. That's when our marriage began unraveling."

"Ted started whining that he felt like he was 40 going on 60," explained Michelle. "He was afraid he would end up with his father's physical ailments, so every time he coughed, he thought he was getting emphysema; and because his father had several heart attacks, he feared he would drop dead before achieving some unfulfilled dreams."

One afternoon Polly's husband, Fred, turned to her and said,

"Most likely, one of us won't be alive in ten years." Polly knew he was referring to himself who, at 51, was overweight, not exercising enough, not eating properly, and suffering intense back pain.

When James' father died suddenly, he started saying, "I don't want to end up dead like my dad with nothing to show for my life." At the time, Lee felt that was an insult to her and their marriage, without recognizing he was sowing the seeds of his midlife crisis.

What's going on? While fast sports cars, prescriptions for Propecia, jars of Rogaine, and sordid affairs leading to broken families are the stuff of cartoons, for club members they can be a living nightmare. Some experts ponder whether midlife crisis might not be a result of American materialism, media hype, and the myth that it is possible to "have it all." Researcher Arnold Kruger believes that acting out a midlife crisis is more frequent when prosperous men have the leisure time to indulge in self-absorption. Nevertheless, the phenomenon is both international and timeless. The French have long referred to midlife as *démon de midi*—the devil that gets into the noonday of their lives when their wives have grown matronly. The Germans call it *Torschlusspanik*, which translates to "closed-door panic"—the pursuit of younger women by middle-aged men seeking a final fling before the gates close. Interestingly, the Chinese ideograph for crisis is made up of the characters for danger and opportunity.

According to Daniel J. Levinson, one of the foremost chroniclers of the human life cycle, upheavals at midlife have been catalogued for thousands of years—although when men did not live as long, either fewer men experienced it or the crisis may have come at an earlier age. Levinson wrote, "Society is now doing better at keeping people healthy after 40. The more difficult problem is to foster psychological well-being and provide the conditions for a satisfying, productive life in middle adult-hood." Today, with male life expectancy closing in on 80, a larger portion of the population is symptomatic so the condition is easier to diagnose. And, as the twenty-first century turned, the biggest generation in history—the baby boomers—were either in the throes of midlife crises or approaching the testy hour.

Yet some studies from other cultures do not support the idea of a universal male midlife crisis, suggesting that only a small percentage of middle-aged men have difficulty coping. Other researchers believe some midlife turmoil is a common marker for men 40 to 45 years of age. Although nobody finds it pleas-ant or flattering, aging is a normal process. No 50-year-old man can compete athletically against someone half his age, nor should he expect to. Graying or balding hair, changes in skin elasticity, even loss of bone mass will affect every man sooner or later. While there are pharmaceuticals that attempt to either slow or assuage some of the inevitable side effects of maturity, there is only so much that can be done to manage serious dis-eases like diabetes, cardiovascular problems, and cancer, which crop up more frequently after 40. In his book *Dare to Be 100*, Dr. Walter Bortz says there is nothing we can do to slow the fact that most of our bodily functions deteriorate about one-half percent per year. Since men in the United States have a higher death rate for the leading causes of death and die on average seven years younger than women, they do have reason for increased anxiety. Yet men are less likely to have medical check-ups or take preventative steps than women, who accept the fact that midlife brings obvious physical changes and that menopause is a time to seek professional advice about their changing bodies.

"Most men are better about getting the oil changed in their car than they are at getting regular health checks," says Patrick Taylor, director of the National Men's Health Foundation in

Allentown, Pennsylvania. In a 1997 survey, the organization found that about a third of the nation's men don't go to their doctor for regular physical exams and 10 percent of the male population has not seen a physician in the last five years. If they did, they might get advice about their changing bodies that would help them cope with symptoms and prevent disease.

Male Menopause

Various labels have attempted to define the sometimes dramatic, sometimes more veiled, changes men undergo between 40 and 60. Dr. Edmond C. Hallberg termed it "malepause" and also referred to it as the "gray itch." Since "menopause" is derived from the Greek word *menses* and refers to women's monthly cycle, some experts prefer "viropause," *vir* being the Latin prefix for man, while others speak of "andropause," based on *andro*, Greek for man. However, the most common term remains "male menopause." While there is some disagreement as to whether all males experience a midlife crisis, most doctors concur that every man will experience physical changes that include significant hormonal fluctuations—not unlike their counterparts in women, only perhaps not as dramatic. While women have hot flashes as well as the cessation of menses to mark their transition, plus a whole pharmaceutical industry offering pills, patches, and potions to alleviate symptoms and provide hormone replacement, men's changes are more subtle, and there is no established regimen to aid their transition.

By age 55, the amount of testosterone secreted into the normal male bloodstream is significantly lower than it was only ten years earlier. A decrease in testosterone is considered the culprit in an array of symptoms, including a general loss of well-being, fatigue, aching joints, stiff hands, and sleep disturbances. A sudden drop in testosterone may lead to premature aging, and changes in hair growth and skin quality. Some men will even experience a hot flash now and then. Others will feel more irritable, are easier to anger, or become depressed. Reduced interest in sex combined with diminished potency are some of the most emotionally devastating symptoms for a man. This may sound familiar to women because the relationship between a woman's ovaries, estrogen, brain, and pituitary glands is similar to that between a man's testes, testosterone, brain, and pituitary glands. Women normally have an acute menopause because hormones cease relatively quickly; however, testicular function sometimes declines more slowly in men—but not always.

At 40 the normal man will notice areas of his body are shifting, shrinking, and changing. A shirt seems looser around the pectorals, and he may have to buy a larger size of slacks. He may still write "six feet" on forms, but the nurse measures him as five-eleven and a half. Muscle is lost; fat is gained, especially in the abdominal region. Wrinkles map new routes on his face, and his once-perfect vision starts to blur. The lenses of his eyes harden and stiffen causing age-related farsightedness. Forty-five percent of men will have noticeable male-pattern baldness with receding hair or a monk's spot spreading on top of their skull by age 45. A midlife man's skin begins to thin. As the gum line recedes, the phrase "long in the tooth" takes on real meaning. The disks of the spine compress causing both a loss of height as well as back problems. With less synovial fluid to coat the joints, knees begin to stiffen. More pain is inflicted by heel spurs resulting from fallen or compressed foot arches. The brain is also not as nimble as it once was, with memory lapses and forgetfulness becoming more common, although men are less likely to joke about "senior moments" or "early Alzheimer's" than women. Over time there will be less endurance for physical activity, and it will take longer to recover from illness and injuries. This is not a pretty picture, and those are only a few of the most obvious signs of male aging.

After beating more than a billion and a half times by age 40, the miraculous heart will be declining, even though it is usually durable for many years to come. Heart disease is the leading cause of death for American men, although the risks can be greatly lessened by eliminating smoking, reducing heavy alcohol consumption, and controlling cholesterol and other fats in the blood.

There are psychological, medical, chemical, and social explanations for the complex transition all men experience as they reach the statistical half-point in their lives. Nevertheless, some experts suggest that the popular concept of midlife crisis is a myth that results in oversimplified stereotypes with the vast majority of men not suffering any serious disruptions. Just as every human was once an infant, then a toddler, young child, and adolescent, if they live out their lifespan, they evolve through multiple adult stages continuing to old age. The truth is that everyone is aging and everyone is going to die. A woman is slapped with this reality when her menstrual cycle ceases and her hormonal pattern indicates she is no longer fertile. Even if she chooses hormone replacement therapy, she is not going to bear any more children (without major medical intervention) and so she has a direct confrontation with her chemical midlife transition. Men's hormones undergo some parallel alterations, but are harder to pinpoint and thus easier to deny. Social dynamics have to be factored in, including the health of aging family members, job and financial pressures, child-raising issues, and older children leaving the nest. Even world events may force a man to reevaluate his value system and patriotism.

Truth or Excuse? Is Midlife Crisis a Reason to Misbehave?

Midlife crisis has been used to define and excuse naughty activities by men of all ages. Can a man of 21 who cheats on his wife be having a midlife crisis? No, he is far from being middle aged and therefore not in the midst of a midlife crisis. He is, quite simply, behaving badly and looking for an excuse to make his actions more acceptable to himself and his peers. When a man enters his middle years and his wife discovers that he is involved in yet another affair, is he then having a midlife crisis? No, a man with a history of infidelity who continues that modus operandi as he enters midlife is not having a midlife crisis; he is merely doing what comes naturally to him.

A man at any age may be depressed or angry, feel trapped or lonely, want to escape his current responsibility, be dishonest or experiencing an addiction, commit sexual infidelity, or be abusive to his spouse. He may have all or a combination of some of these feelings or actions. The behaviors and emotions themselves do not signal a midlife crisis, although their presence has the potential to estrange him from his spouse at any stage of their marriage. But a man who enters middle age and suddenly finds himself depressed, angry, trapped, lonely, in love with someone other than his wife, or feeling the urge to run from all responsibility is likely to be embarking on a typical midlife crisis.

Unsure of whether their mate's condition will create a temporary or terminal rift in their marriage, many women log online to try to diagnose the situation. Is it something they did? Is there anything they can do? Maybe it is something else—anything else! Will it go away? How long will it take? There are no easy answers, but there are clues to who might be having a midlife crisis. Here are representative queries from postings on the Midlife Wives Club website:

"David turned 50 yesterday," posted Miriam. "He is in another state celebrating his birthday with his parents and friends, without me or our son. This is the third vacation he has taken by himself in the past seven months, and when he is home, he studies religious books and never does anything with us. He tells me if I want to go out, I should find a friend. David's been this way for almost a year now, and I am at the end of my rope."

"Last night Shane announced he wants a divorce," said Melissa her first time online. "We've been together for 12 years, and have three kids, ages ten, four, and one. The problem is that he's only 26! Could he be having a midlife crisis since we got together so young? He was 14, and I was 17. He says he feels like he missed out on something. I don't think he's been unfaithful yet, but he has a lot of other symptoms. He is angry at me for no good reason, he's depressed (although he won't admit it), and he moved out to think about what was best for him. Now, two weeks later, he says he wants a divorce. The only reason he gives is there might be something 'more' or 'better' out there for him. So is it possible to have a midlife crisis at only 26?"

"After 25 years of marriage, Gavin made a career change, and we moved to Florida," wrote Candy. "It took me eight months to transfer my job, sell the house, and move the family. By the time I got to the Sunshine State, Gavin had taken up with a tramp who was married with three kids. After one month living with this mess, I moved back home and found myself jobless for the first time in my life."

So which of these men is probably having a midlife crisis: David, Shane, or Gavin? While all three men are acting in a way that threatens their marriages, David and Gavin are both middle-aged and so their sudden lifestyle changes could indicate an impending midlife crisis. Yet, anyone at any age can be unhappy with their current life and responsibilities and many marriages fail with younger couples. So while Shane, at 26, has the same symptoms, he is excluded from the midlife crisis category.

Trigger Unhappy: Rating Your Mate's Risk Factors

Sometimes the crisis heats up slowly over time. Day after day a man looks in the mirror and sees himself getting older—perhaps he looks astonishingly like his father or uncle—and he may feel the urge to prove he is still a virile man by making a play for a younger woman. Doubts about his abilities as a lover, father, and breadwinner surface, and insecurities he thought he had conquered after adolescence break the glassy surface of his stable life like stones tossed into a placid pond. These may be mere ripples that cause some consternation but soon sink to the bottom, life moving on much as it was. Other times boulders create waves that threaten to engulf him and his whole family.

These swells—commonly known as triggers—can sink a marriage. However, it is not the trigger itself that is the cause of the crisis, but how each man reacts to his particular trigger. A man might have coped with a testy teenager or a job downsizing at a less vulnerable time in his life, but when he is feeling old and tired, he may react out of fear or anger, which escalates the issues and may result in a battle royal with his son or cause the loss of his job. Also, he may have the reserve fortitude to deal with one issue—for example, the illness of a parent—but when several triggers mount, his emotional savings account becomes precariously low.

One of the most well-known tools to measure stress is the Social Readjustment Rating Scale developed by Holmes and Rahe more than 30 years ago, which gives points to various social factors. Scores of more than 300 indicate an 80 percent chance of psychological or medical illness, while scores in the 150 to 299 range put someone at a 50 percent risk, although even scores less than 150 still suggest a 30 percent risk. If midlife insecurities that may weaken previous immunities are factored in, a man who could have breezed through a job change in his thirties may crumble in his late forties.

The following are the social factors on this scale that may affect midlife men as well as the points assigned to them:

Death of spouse	100
Divorce	73
Marital separation	65
Jail term	63
Death of close family member	63
Personal injury or illness	53
New marriage	50
Fired from work	47
Marital reconciliation	45
Retirement	45
Change in family member's health	44
Sex difficulties	39
Addition to family	39
Business readjustment	39
Change in financial status	38
Death of close friend	37
Change to a different line of work	36
Change in number of marital arguments	35
Mortgage or loan over $10,000	31
Foreclosure of mortgage or loan	30
Change in work responsibilities	29
Trouble with in-laws	29
Outstanding personal achievement	28
Spouse begins or stops work	26

Change in living conditions	25
Revision of personal habits	24
Trouble with boss	23
Change in work hours, conditions	20
Change in residence	20
Change in recreational habits	19
Change in church activities	19
Change in social activities	18
Mortgage or loan under $10,000	17
Change in sleeping habits	16
Change in number of family gatherings	15
Change in eating habits	15
Vacation	13
Christmas season	12
Minor violations of the law	11

When club members added up the scores for their men, the results were not unexpected. Sasha's husband topped the chart with 371 life change units, which included 78 points for the birth of twins on top of troubles at work, relocating to another state, and leaving behind his network of friends and extended family.

Amanda gave Colin the lowest score—80—in the poll. "In his case, boredom had set in. He was looking for something more exciting, and boy, did he get his wish!" Since they split up, Colin has experienced more than his fair share of stress. His father died, his garage was burglarized, he crashed his car, gave up his job, moved into the city, and accepted a temporary position. Then he started a new business, but had trouble financing it, so his debts increased rapidly. "But he'll be okay," Amanda said sarcastically, "because I'm sure that his new 21-year-old girlfriend understands everything better than I ever could."

Most of the spouses' scores hovered in the 230 to 275 range.

Lauren pointed out that "merely turning 40 or 50 should be on the stress test. For us it began about two months prior to Nick's fiftieth birthday. Just before that a male friend who was two years older than him died. Then his dad was diagnosed with cancer. Next he was laid off and began to drink more than usual on the weekends." Lauren knew tension was building. She knew the midlife issue was looming when he begged her not to tell people her age. "Although I always looked younger, I'm actually two years his senior and I have always boasted about my age. Five years ago that didn't bother him, but suddenly he became furious if I mentioned it."

Super Stressors

One of the classic triggers for a major crisis is a parent's death. Twenty-eight percent of our polltakers reported the death of a close family member. A person between the ages of 40 to 44 has a 74 percent chance of having a living mother, but it drops to 34 percent between the ages of 55 to 59. Because men die earlier, only 57 percent of people between 40 and 44 have a living father, and this falls to 31 percent among those 45 to 49.

"It started with his father's passing," Lee explained. "James fell apart in the hospital room when his father was declared dead." All Lee's maternal instincts kicked in, and she tried to put her own problems aside and be there for her husband. She thought it best to go along with whatever he wanted, which included having his headstrong mother move into their home. "If I thought it was bad before this, I soon learned what hell is like. Within a month he began sneaking around with a co-worker."

Seven percent of our polltakers reported that their mates had lost a significant friend. Typically, a midlife man scans the obituaries for men who died at ages similar to his own and once in a while sees the names of people he knows. While the death of a parent is always hard, death of a contemporary brings an icy awareness of one's own mortality. "One of George's closest friends was diagnosed with lung cancer and died within six months. He was only 43, a non-smoker, marathon runner, and seemed healthy as a horse," Megan said. "Two months after the funeral, George didn't want to be married any longer."

Death of a dream is another trigger—or any serious job-related pressure. More than 48 percent of the male spouses in our poll had major changes in work responsibilities, while about 20 percent changed jobs. Four percent were fired, and a considerable 27 percent had business adjustments to make. Changes in work hours accounted for 32 percent, and 13 percent were experiencing difficulties with their bosses. While a man might cope with one of these modifications in his life, the stressors mount when several pile on at once, especially since he may no longer see an endless horizon.

Michelle reported that Ted's goal was to become a vice president in his company before he retired. "He had a couple of bad performance appraisals that he blamed on me. I don't know how I could have been the cause of his not being able to get that promotion, but that is how he saw it."

"Job problems were a huge issue for Gabe," Emily* agreed during a discussion online. "As his high-tech company began to lay off more people, he became deeply concerned." Gabe, who never attended college, had moved into management by merit. "He didn't believe he could start over competing with the 'young dudes.'" He also didn't think that Emily understood daily pressures and began confiding in a female colleague who soon became the other woman in their marriage.

After Megan's husband, George, lost his friend, he started to reevaluate his whole life. George, who ran his own computer programming business, had always put in long hours, but then sold his company for megabucks. "You would have thought this indecent amount of money—plus the time to enjoy it— would have made him happy," Megan said, "but the opposite was true. He hated our small house, his old car, and thought new ones would fill the void. So, presto! We were rich. We found our dream house and bought it for cash. We furnished it with everything he always wanted including a pool table and giant screen television added to the six other TVs and four VCRs, as well as a BMW 540. The reality was that nothing satisfied him because he wasn't happy with himself." George became increasingly withdrawn, countering Megan's every attempt to talk to him with the ubiquitous "nothing." Something had gone terribly wrong, even though he realized his dream. In fact, his outstanding achievement caused his life change units to rise considerably with a business readjustment; alterations in financial status, work responsibilities, hours, and conditions; a new home; new recreational activities; and other different personal habits. Then, when his friend died, George's stress score soared over 300.

Unlike George, most men have come to grips with the fact that they won't be a millionaire by 40 or 50, or maybe ever. They won't be on a bestseller list or have a hit record or accept an Oscar or Emmy. Some of these dreams were never realistic; others, like earning a promotion, building a home, owning a lakeside cabin, getting an advanced degree, may have been more attainable, but the older the man gets, the further out of reach they may become because time seems to be running out. Anything that reminds him that the rungs on the ladder are being cut before he can climb them may elicit more critical symptoms.

Even though Megan's husband's score was one of the highest, she believed this test may not reflect some economic realities.

"Sure it's stressful to have a change in working conditions, but is a promotion or making a pile of money really as tough as having to accept a lower paying job and worrying about making ends meet? I don't think one can say the stress of deciding what TV to buy is the equivalent of worrying about having enough money to feed the children this month."

His Turn: Pedro

"I went from a military career to civilian life, never anticipating the catastrophic effect of that change. In a way it was a death because the only way of life I'd ever known was over. I no longer had a high rank, nobody saluted, and to make matters worse, I was taking orders from people who were young enough to be my children!"

Some couples try to reinvent their lives together by encouraging one or the other to change jobs, go back to school, have another child, adopt the child they always wanted, take a financial risk, or move to another location. In doing so, however, they are invoking risk factors. Thirty-eight percent of our group said their men had changed work either by taking a new position, retiring, or getting back into the job market once their children were older. Moving to a new home affected 23 percent of the polltakers and, while some stayed in their own community, a long-distance move automatically added additional adjustments including changes in social life, how often they saw their family, and their general living environment.

Mallory first logged on in October 2001 with the ultimate stress-induced midlife crisis. "On September 11, my husband,

Eugene, who works close to the Twin Towers, was one of those running for his life. Along the way, he met up with two women, sisters, who couldn't get home because the trains were not running. We live in the city and have a car, so he made it his mission to get them home safely, which took 12 hours. Even though I knew he was okay, I was furious with him because I was freaked by everything that had happened and knew some people who were missing. He calmed me down by saying, 'If you were the one stranded, I would have wanted someone to get you home safely.' For the next few weeks, he was angry, bitter, and lashed out at me. He was furious at the world and wanted to shoot everything in his path. Early in October, he broke down and cried and that seemed to bring him some relief. I thought he was just venting his rage for the despicable acts of the terrorists."

Over the next weeks, Mallory slowly unfolded more of her story. Eugene developed a friendship with one of the sisters, and Mallory began to find her phone number on his cell phone bill, appearing at 6:15 AM—right after he left for work—and 11:30 PM—when he walked the dog. Each call would be 30 minutes or more. Eugene began to complain about their relationship and withdraw. After Mallory joined the Midlife Wives Club, she urged him to find a counselor, even going so far as to make an appointment for him, but he canceled it because he was afraid he would learn "we aren't right for each other."

After some cyber-snooping, Mallory discovered he had changed his password to the other woman's name, and the two were having a flirtatious e-mail correspondence with phrases like "Sweet dreams honey," "Woke up thinking about you," and "What would you like for Christmas?" When Mallory confronted him, Eugene blasted her for invading his privacy. By January 2002, Eugene had moved out. Midlife Wives Club members distraught over Mallory's predicament counseled her not to underestimate the impact of 9/11 on Eugene, given how close he was to Ground Zero. Some suggested he was suffering from post-traumatic stress disorder, or, at the very least, this overload triggered his midlife crisis.

Fly Away Home: Rebelling Against Parental Responsibility

Midlife parenting issues overwhelm some of the mates of club members. Three major changes can upset the family applecart. Most typically, middle-aged parents are struggling with adolescent children. A youngster's smiley face is replaced by a teenager's sullen glare, and parental comments are met with the adolescent's surly "whatevers"—or worse. Even the most sanguine parent can't help but feel miffed; others feel rejected at a time when their own self-esteem is declining. Also, surprise premenopausal pregnancies or the success of complicated infertility treatments may deliver demanding infant bundles to midlife parents. Or, a woman who married a man a number of years older than herself may conceive their first or subsequent children as he reaches his middle years. An addition to the family affected over 11 percent of our poll takers. A baby alters sleep patterns and other social interactions, adding more points. Finally, adult children, who were expected to be independent, may be staying home longer or returning to the nest due to personal problems or difficult economic conditions. Since more than two million American grandparents are raising their grandchildren, many middle-aged adults are saddled with this unforeseen responsibility.

Grace believed their adolescent children's behavior contributed to Roger's need to escape. "He felt that they had too much of my attention and should be left to learn life's lessons through the consequences of their actions. I sometimes thwarted impending disasters by helping them out, so he felt he was losing control. He also wanted time for himself and became aggravated by the boys' normal noise and messes."

Emily said that Gabe was bent out of shape because their eldest child, who was entering his senior year of high school, was hanging out with girls, driving everywhere, and acting cool. "He envied the kid's freedom. Soon he started behaving like his son's older brother instead of his father. If only he knew how foolish he looked!" Emily thought the term "empty nest syndrome" was one way women expressed their changing status. "Women are more likely to define themselves as mothers so when the chicks fly the coop, they feel the emptiness more acutely and are willing to admit this loss. While fathers are not immune, this time in life brings a reassessment of where they've been, where they are, and where they want to be."

After Ginger's second son was born, she and Ernst thought their family was complete and she had a tubal ligation. As they were getting older, both decided they made a mistake, and she had the surgery reversed. Sadly, she had two miscarriages and two ectopic pregnancies, which meant she could no longer bear children. "Two days after the last pregnancy ended, Ernst wanted to go deer hunting. When I said I needed him, he yelled at me, saying that I knew he had planned the hunting trip for a year." He stayed home, but Ginger knew he resented it. A few months later, when he was repairing the car, she brought him a cold drink and said, "I wish you needed me more." Ernst got out from under the car and said he wasn't sure he wanted to stay married to her.

His Turn: Adam

"After my son was born, my wife and I went from very close to the darkest period in our marriage. Just when I was desperate for more freedom, she needed me to accept more responsibility, but I wasn't in the mood to make sacrifices in my lifestyle. That's when I started looking around for potential other women."

When Vanda's daughter had an unexpected pregnancy, she moved home just as Vanda's marriage was disintegrating. "Somehow Oliver found a way to blame me for this too. When the baby was born, it made sense for my daughter to continue living with me because my daughter could be home during the day and work the night shift when I could cover for her." Oliver used this as an excuse to move out, saying not only wasn't he ready to be a grandfather, but he also couldn't tolerate having a baby in the house ruining his peace and quiet.

Vigor Mortis: Impotency at Midlife

Almost every man realizes his sexual potency is waning, and some are more alarmed than others to find their interest in sex is reduced. Our poll was taken by women on behalf of their husbands, so we might have gotten a different result if the men had taken it themselves. However, a mate knows when sexual issues arise, and 30 percent reported these in their relationship. Many men develop anxieties when it takes longer to have an erection, then their fears exacerbate the problem. According to the Bayer pharmaceutical company, over 30 million American men and more than 140 million worldwide suffer from erectile dysfunction. Impotence probably affects more than half of men over the age of 40 with the incidence increasing with age. Sometimes they blame their partner or fantasize about having sex with others because it is easier to claim their wife is undesirable rather than face their inadequacy.

Bonnie admitted sex hadn't been thrilling for many years. When she approached Nigel, he said she was no longer appealing and suggested swinging. "When I balked, he placed an Internet ad for a bisexual female he could master."

For more than 30 years, Sonia thought she had the perfect marriage. "Jordan and I hardly ever fought about anything and our sex life was fine until he started having erectile difficulties. We were both delighted when the doctor prescribed Viagra. For a few months we were both satisfied, but then our sex life became nonexistent." Sonia's approach was to avoid any confrontation that would make Jordan feel worse because every other part of their relationship was satisfactory—or so she thought. Soon much of what he said didn't add up. A few quick errands stretched to hours, he avoided spending free time with the family, he ended their traditional Saturday night outings, he even cut back on their vacation to work on remodeling projects. Fleeting suspicions of another woman surfaced, but Sonia had no proof, and it seemed Jordan was more tired and discouraged than a Don Juan. After a year without sex, Jordan went on a business trip, and Sonia called the pharmacy to get a copy of his prescriptions for the year. "Knowing we hadn't had sex since August of 2000, I knew that if there were any Viagra prescriptions past the first one, I would have my answer. Well you guessed it, there were many!"

Relationship problems escalate with more frequent arguments over sex, love, and intimacy. The wife may complain about not feeling cherished enough, not getting enough sex, not having enough time together to talk, while the man may want to avoid any discussion that will expose his worries about his prowess. "Loss of potency is scary," says Dr. Harvey Sternbach of UCLA. "Low testosterone can be tied to a growing sense of figurative and literal impotence, and therefore tied to doing things to compensate."

Lee's husband had performance problems early on due to a serious back injury. "As far as I was concerned, that would never have changed the way I loved him." Nevertheless James was frustrated, and even more so when it didn't improve after surgery. Lee hinted he should see a urologist, but he never told her that he had. Then she opened a drawer and found a prescription for Viagra. "At first I was glad, thinking he wanted to make love to me, but when I mentioned it sweetly, he was annoyed I had found it. That's when it occurred to me that he intended to try it with someone else, not me."

Thea said Burt exhibited andropause symptoms for at least five years before he left home. "He had a low sex drive, impotency, and fatigue. I finally pressured him into seeing a urologist who did a testosterone level, which turned out to be extremely low. He tried a few testosterone injections, but I guess it was more than his ego could handle, because after the third, he refused to go back." Thea believed it soon became a double-edged sword. The low testosterone led to a fear of intimacy. The combination of the physical problems led to psychological ones. "It was a vicious cycle that we couldn't resolve."

His Turn: Stan*

"I'm 38 and I thought I was a happily married man. Right now, I'm miserable. Last night I stepped on a scale and was way overweight. I recently started working out at a gym, but the pounds don't come off the way they used to. In fact, nothing is working out the way it used to. I feel frustrated most of the time and yesterday a friend asked me why I've given up some hobbies we had in common.

"Okay, you guessed it, I have fallen for someone much younger. When I look in the mirror, I see that I am not a spring chicken anymore, but she seems interested, although I am not sure why. Last night I slept only two hours. Being with this girl is not an option, but I feel like I am living a lie with her and my wife. I wish I could tell my wife how I feel, but I can't put the stress on her. So I have to bottle this up, although I feel like I'll burst and the worms will come crawling out."

Midlife Crisis Quiz

Vulnerability factors: How many does your man exhibit?

- ❑ He is between 40 and 60 (give or take a few years).
- ❑ He is on either side of his fortieth (or fiftieth) birthday.
- ❑ He is showing concerns about getting "old."
- ❑ He has bought a more youthful wardrobe.
- ❑ He is coloring his hair or trying a trendier cut.
- ❑ He has started working out.

- He reminisces about his teen years or "when he was younger."

- He listens to romantic songs from his dating years.

- He talks about his "first love" and wonders "what if?"

- He yearns for a sportier vehicle (or has bought one).

- He doesn't find enjoyment in the usual leisure-time activities.

- He wants to do something adventuresome like hang gliding or auto racing.

- He is bored with life.

- He questions the meaning of his life.

- He is dissatisfied with his job or career.

- He feels trapped by responsibilities or obligations to others.

- He has financial problems.

- He worries about the future.

- He suddenly wants another child.

- He is unhappy that the children are grown and on their own.

- He has some major health problems.

- He has experienced the death of a parent, close friend, or other family member.

- He is frequently nervous and/or irritable.

- He criticizes his wife and marriage.

- He is not interested in sex.

❑ He is occasionally impotent.

❑ He feels inadequate.

❑ He says he loves his wife but isn't "in love" with her.

❑ He is uncharacteristically abusive.

❑ He has been recently divorced. (For those dating a midlife man, the crisis may not be over yet!)

❑ He worries about everything to excess.

❑ His sleeping habits have changed.

❑ He drinks more or is experimenting with drugs.

❑ He feels that life no longer has any purpose.

❑ He is concerned about death and dying.

❑ He talks about suicide in the near or far future.

Scoring: Less than 5 may indicate normal aging issues. 6–10 indicate more worrisome issues. 11–15 suggest he has some serious midlife issues. 16 or more indicate a crisis is on the immediate horizon.

Some of these signs are more serious than others. The next chapter will help sort out the red flags as well as offer clues as to what prompts a man to take a detour from a formerly happy way of life.

CHAPTER 3

Warning Signs and Flashing Signals: When to Worry—and When to Relax

Between the desire
And the spasm
Between the potency
And the existence
Between the essence
And the descent
Falls the Shadow

—T. S. Eliot, written 1925, age 47

Many women sense something is not right, but they have no proof. They are looking for answers, but also hoping they won't find them. They know enough about midlife issues to be concerned, but many pray that "midlife crisis" does not apply to them. Conversely, everyone suffers some insecurities about aging. It's normal to be irritated by new aches and pains, signs of forgetfulness, the appearance of gray hairs or bald spots. An illness may exacerbate these concerns—at least temporarily—and upheavals at work add a different sort of stress. When a true crisis is building, the symptoms increase until they can no longer be ignored.

"I was starting to become suspicious about a bunch of signs, but I didn't understand them until I found the Midlife Wives Club site and read the advice to newcomers," Marina wrote online. "Walker is a classic case. He started to withdraw from us about a year ago. After his father passed, he slowly became more distant and started staying away from home. Frankly, I didn't mind, because when he was around, he was angry all the time."

Still, pinning down the exact symptoms of a midlife crisis can be like punching Jell-O. As Len D. McMillan, author of *An Owner's Guide to Male Midlife Crisis*, noted, "A man in the throes of midlife crisis may be depressed, anxious, fearful, and obsessive all at once. He feels unhappy with his lot in life, with his work, and his spouse. He doubts the choices he has made and begins to dwell on how he may never attain the pinnacles of success and fulfillment he always imagined were within his reach. He feels inadequate and begins to fear his own aging and death. To cope with these feelings, he may turn to sexual fantasy, alcohol, drugs, infidelity, or other escapes."

Daisy first noticed Arnold's lack of attention to their home. "He used to love spending weekends on a household project or working in the yard. Suddenly he let everything go and started hanging out with a single male friend." At first Daisy didn't mind, but then as the grass grew higher and the car needed tuning, he expected her to take care of it. "I worked full time, and we have three children, so I resented not having his help." Soon a cycle started. Daisy made nasty comments and Arnold reacted by slamming the door and leaving. Then he would start arguments so he would have a reason to take off to be with the guys. "I didn't figure out it was midlife crisis until I became sick physically and mentally and went to seek help for myself."

Zoë was disturbed when Brian stopped holding her at night.

"He was always a touchy-feely man. Even if we were angry with each other, he would cuddle in the middle of the night. But when the changes began, he kept to his side of the bed."

Bonnie couldn't understand why Nigel refused to take her to his twentieth class reunion. Spouses were invited, but he told her that few were going. "The truth was he didn't want to be seen with me."

"Three years before anything dramatic happened, Sven started complaining about his job. That escalated into complaints about everything," reported Nora as she was trying to figure out when their marriage started to unravel. "He no longer liked my friends, our neighbors, even had nasty words about the kid who sacks groceries at the supermarket." At first Nora figured he was having a bad day, then she chalked it up to the fact that he was drinking a few more beers every night and going to bed two hours early exhausted.

None of these women suspected midlife crisis, but they knew that something was going awry. Cecilia warned that a man may be experiencing the midlife malfunction if he exhibits three or more of the following symptoms:

- He can't remember why he got married.

- He forgets that this started out as a partnership. He thinks he can resign whenever he pleases.

- He rewrites what you considered a good marriage by stating, "We were never happy."

- He says he can't commit to this marriage any longer but wants to begin again with someone else, or start a new family, or go into debt for a Lamborghini Diablo.

- He wants what he can't have and doesn't want whatever he knows he can have.

- He finds himself thinking, "Responsibility bad, spontaneity good."

- He develops an optic nerve-to-brain malfunction that leads him to believe he is as young as the person he is looking at (usually named Brandi or Dawn or Tiffany).

- He thinks that avoiding the present automatically eradicates the past and changes the future.

- He begins to talk like Garbo ("I vant to be alone") while acting like Richard Gere in *American Gigolo*.

- He starts blaming you, saying, "This is your fault, anyway" or "I wouldn't have done it if you hadn't forced me into it."

- When you criticize him, he snaps, "You're not my mother!"

- He makes excuses for his behavior because it is "my life and nobody else's."

Objects in Mirror Are Closer Than They Appear: Understanding His Behavior

Some women begin to worry even though their husbands may not have acted on their impulses. LaVonne wrote, "I don't know why I feel impending doom, but I do. Billy used to be the steady one and I was the flighty one; now our roles seem reversed. He is having trouble sleeping and spending more time on his computer—even getting up at dawn to log on—and less with the family. Maybe he's having a computer romance, but I don't think so. If he's having an affair, he is very clever because his schedule is the same. I know he's unhappy about his looks. He even bought men's hair coloring. But then I dye my hair, so I ask myself, 'What's wrong with that?' " Although LaVonne remained uneasy, she tried to run a calm household and be loving with Billy. "He may be depressed and doesn't know it, but when I suggested this, he blew up and slammed the door for the first time. Does any of this make sense?" she asked the club.

Lonnie also tried to make sense of inconclusive symptoms. "Travis will be 40 next year, and we have been married for 11 years. He has always been a loyal, devoted, dependable guy. Over the past eight months or so, he has withdrawn emotionally and isolated himself with bizarre but harmless activities. Last summer, it was intensive tanning. He would come home from work and immediately change into a swimsuit and go lie in the backyard. He spent all weekend in the sun, which was weird and uncharacteristic. Then he started reading astrology and finding justification for his behavior in his horoscope. Soon his job started taking precedence over our family, which again isn't like him. He was always the come-home-at-five kind of guy before this." When Lonnie attempted to talk with Travis, he admitted he found more satisfaction at work because other employees looked up to him and sought his advice. At home he had always been more passive and let Lonnie run the show. "It never bothered him until now, but he says he feels 'smothered.' Is he depressed or is it a midlife crisis? Is there really a difference? Will it get worse? What should I do?" Lonnie begged the club members. "Should I back off and let him be in control?"

Betty, married 18 years to Jonathan, noticed some drastic changes. "First he gave up several of his hobbies, claiming they didn't interest him any longer. He used to only want family cars, but started shopping for a Jaguar convertible. Then he voiced fears of ending up like his dad even though he just turned 40. Due to finances, he didn't buy a sports car; instead he splurged on a casual wardrobe and rarely wore his suits and ties. He complained that our daughter, then ten, was growing up so fast and said he wanted more children, knowing full well that I'd had a hysterectomy." Jonathan then spent weeks on the Internet looking for high school classmates he never cared about before. Out loud he would wonder if he missed something prior to their marriage. Then came the relationship with the other woman. "She isn't even younger than me, but is free to have fun with him whenever he wants."

Steep Grade Ahead

Men who don't see themselves as walking clichés experience a form of denial. Although a woman may be slow to perceive the symptoms, their man also refuses to be categorized. He is *not* a typical case. He is *different*. *His* love story is unique!

Chloe wrote, "Vic has been acting weird lately. Now he tells me he is going to get a motorcycle. Talk about your typical midlife crisis move. I am not allowed any input into this decision. What should I do or say?"

Grace told her, "You're lucky if he stops at a motorcycle. Sure, this might be the first sign, but it also might be the most radical thing he does. So don't flip out. Roger swears he is not having a midlife crisis. He says he's thought long and hard and he doesn't want to be married anymore, that he's in love with someone else and wants to spend the rest of his life with his 'soulmate.' He thinks life is too short not to take the opportunity."

Roger started resenting the ties of family and complained that Grace put their children before him, then he began shopping for motorcycles. When she worried about safety, he went out and bought a sports car without discussing it with her. "What hurt the most was that he stopped giving me affectionate kisses. When I suggested midlife crisis, he denied it. Now he's left me for a woman in her twenties."

The Bigger the Boy . . .

As trite as it sounds, many club members report that boy toys loomed large in the lives of their big boys. He starts dropping words like 750 cc engines, 20,000 rpm redline, all-time four-wheel drive, global positioning, six-speed manual transmission, nautical miles, and naming numbers of cylinders or turbos. Is it a coincidence that fantasy brand names—Bugatti, Lamborghini, Maserati, Ferrari—have an erotic lilt as they roll off the tongue? Just as teen males obsess about their dream car, the midlife man feels a compulsion to reel in a trophy vehicle. Depending on income and interests, they may become enamored of cars, motorcycles, boats, or airplanes, even sign up for daredevil activities like rock climbing. By taking to the open road or the sea or the sky, the midlife man renews adolescent sensations with thrill-seeking behavior.

Pat's husband purchased a motorcycle a year after he received the infamous "Gramps" T-shirt. "Money was tight so this wasn't the time for a capricious purchase. After Frank joined the local motorcycle club, he decided he needed a newer, bigger model." Now that they had two motorcycles, Pat thought it wiser to join in than fight the inevitable so she took a class to get her motorcycle license. "I dropped out when I envisioned myself hamburger on the highway."

Midlife men may not have the same sense of self-preservation. After racing a Ferrari cross country at outlandish speeds, writer P. J. O'Rourke recounted, "There is no more profound feeling of control over one's destiny that I have ever experienced than to drive a Ferrari down a public road at 130 miles an hour."

Although a renewed interest in fast women and even faster cars is laughable to some, club members who have lived through their mate's self-indulgence—often at the expense of their budgets, if not their marriages—don't find the jokes amusing. "Right after telling me and our daughter that we'd have to tighten our belts because Archer was only getting part-time work, I discovered that he spent thirteen thousand dollars on a Harley!" said a furious Marlene. "When business picked up, Archer spent three times that on a souped-up Camaro so packed with speed that it is a lethal weapon on the road. Why couldn't he see that the car was like a neon sign flashing: 'pathetic old man trying to look young'?"

After saving for years, when Evie and Robert finally could afford a second car, he insisted on a racy Alfa Romeo. "I thought that would satisfy Robert, but then he was on to new clothes, better grooming and exercise, all items he hadn't cared tuppence for before."

"Colin's first boy toy was the classic red convertible," Amanda told the club. "He loved showing it off, and taking our daughters for a spin in it." Amanda described how Colin, who had just turned 37, was dissatisfied with his factory job and the repairs he had to make to their house on weekends. She suggested they join a social club and this turned into more of a success than she planned. "He turned back into the ladies' man he was when I met him: charming, funny, a big tease. I was always coming into the room finding a girl on his knee, but at home he acted sullen and withdrawn."

Lois' partner was notoriously cheap, so she became wary when he whipped out his credit card and ordered a new laptop computer from a catalog. "This was Kevin's first impulsive purchase. And do you know what my reaction was?" Lois asked as she reviewed her stupidity in hindsight. "I spent the next two weeks setting the computer up, installing software and fonts, transferring our files, and making it exactly like the home computer so he would have everything precisely the way he liked it. Then, as soon as it was fully functional, he dumped me!"

Barb said that Ben "went through recreational vehicles, tents, gardening, aviaries, show dogs, sports cars, motorbikes, scooters, sailing boats, canal boats—the list goes on and on—but nothing made him content. I went along with every whim thinking that adventures were good and we could share them. Alas, it wasn't to be."

Other men become obsessed with their appearance—balding remedies crop up on the bathroom counter, as do hair and beard dyes. A few go in for hair implants or toupees. The American Society of Plastic Surgeons reports that in 2000 more than one million men—an all-time high—had cosmetic surgery. Eyelid surgery was the most popular operation followed by liposuction, nose reshaping, and male breast reduction. The cosmetic industry is also getting a boon thanks to male baby boomers who are incorporating hair color, skin moisturizers, toning lotions, anti-aging creams, even makeup into their routine ablutions. Roger Selbert, a Santa Monica–based trend analyst, reports that "Men today are concerned about their appearance out of necessity: for work, for relationships, and for self-esteem. This has changed dramatically over the last 50 years. Men have to look better at work. It's a competitive environment, with younger guys coming up all the time. There still is age discrimination."

Use Low Gear: The Search for Answers

While all men age and have some common experiences, Midlife Wives Club members search for clues as to why their mates fell so hard. What was in their background or personality that sparked a major episode? As they compare notes, they find many common traits.

Polly saw Fred's downfall as a complex stew that had been on the back burner for many years. "We had marriage issues that needed work, but they were at a subtle level and were outweighed by the love and other good stuff in the marriage. As soon as he started to realize he was growing older, he took everything harder, especially his father's death and some new physical problems, and soon he was fighting a feeling of hopelessness." Fred found escape with his first impulsive purchase, a sailboat. The next distraction from his tumultuous feelings was the other woman. "I believe the ones who avoid midlife crisis either have fewer or less intense versions of those issues or may be willing to face them and work through them rather than blaming others for their problems or looking for quick cures," wrote Polly.

Many members felt their husbands had never been allowed to express their emotions as youngsters. "All those years of acting out a role to please others took their toll on Ted," Michelle suggested. "Anger toward a parent had been simmering for his whole life, but he never dared express it. When it boiled over, I was the one scalded."

Colleen believed that when Rory faced opportunity mixed with adulation, the combination was potent. After they moved to Japan, he was surrounded by admiring young women. "For a short, 50-something balding man who was not as attractive in North America as he was in Asia, the temptation proved irresistible."

Another factor Colleen mentioned—that seems a familiar Midlife Wives Club theme—is marrying because of a pregnancy. "Since we had to get married, Rory felt he had missed something. So when an opportunity presented itself 30 years later, he was determined to make up for lost time."

Here is a list of the most common traits or life experiences of midlife crisis men (from the members' viewpoints):

- Married as a teen or in early twenties
- Had no serious girlfriends before marriage
- Had first child in teens
- First child was an unplanned pregnancy
- Pregnancy was the cause of marriage
- Experienced the death of a parent in childhood or before age 30
- Experienced the death of a parent at midlife
- Often overworks to meet financial obligations, and is stressed
- Always put others before himself in the past
- Has an inability to say no
- Has low self-esteem
- Has a dysfunctional birth family
- Has serious problems with mother or father that persist into adulthood
- Experienced childhood neglect and/or abuse
- Had serious problems as a child
- Has problems with one of his children, particularly an adolescent
- Has substance-abusing parents
- Is a substance abuser—most often alcohol
- Has passive-aggressive tendencies

- Is non-confrontational, at least on the surface

- Is highly judgmental

- Is hypercritical

- Has a rigid sense of right and wrong

- Has difficulty accepting varying points of view

Remember that couples can quarrel, have problems with their children and in-laws, weather illness and career changes, and grieve for a loved one without disastrous consequences. By understanding what men experience, it is easier to differentiate normal reactions to life's inevitable ups and downs from severe symptoms that can wreck a family.

Dr. Alon Gratch, a psychotherapist who works primarily with men, has studied why most men—in contrast to women—find it so difficult to be open with their feelings. In his book, *If Men Could Talk*, Gratch isolates seven male attributes that he believes are responsible for this difference.

The first is *shame*, which covers why men often avoid emotional discussions, and also why boys are not supposed to cry. When a man feels his performance is inadequate, Gratch says he may project his disappointment onto his partner by finding fault with her. Club members often mention that their husbands criticize their appearance or belittle abilities, but what they don't always understand is that this behavior stems from their man's sense of inadequacy. Sadly, these nasty comments peak at a time when women may be most vulnerable, because they are aging and dealing with the lack of self-confidence that comes with wrinkles and weight gain. When the women accuse the men of being cruel or controlling, the men claim the women are overly sensitive, and defensive and toxic fights ensue. Conversely, consorting with younger women helps men project a younger image on themselves, which brings a new destructive element to a relationship. But if a man could have confronted his real feelings by telling his wife, "I'm worried about being passed up for a promotion," the marital rift, as well as the self-deception, might have been avoided.

Another attribute is *emotional absence*, in which a man doesn't understand what he is feeling and often is resistant to talking about it. When a wife tries to learn how her spouse is feeling, he often responds, "I think . . ." avoiding an emotional response. Many club members complain that they had no idea what was going on in their husbands' heads until faced with a real crisis. Some women have been able to break through the barrier of emotional absence by engaging first in the intellectual discussions, then gently leading the man toward discussing some deeper—and possibly scarier—feelings. Club members also claim counseling at a strategic time assisted fruitful communication.

Masculine insecurity is what men keep hidden under their fortified, tough-guy personas. Deep down many men are tired of being on top—in the boardroom as well as the bedroom—but when they realize that is what they are thinking, they feel less masculine and may act more competitive to prove they really don't want to be coddled. This same attribute also can lead to anxiety about a man's sexual performance. If a man has a few brushes with impotence, he feels mounting pressure to perform, but this added stress leads to more problems that become a vicious circle. Midlife may heighten masculine insecurity when men begin to wonder whether all the striving was worth it or whether they will ever meet their youthful objectives. They might also fear that their naturally slower sexual response is the prelude to permanent impotence. Gratch discusses how insecurity is affected by the masculine-feminine split that occurs when the wife complains her husband is a "passive, submissive doormat, and the husband feels that the wife is a control freak and a cold fish" or when the couple takes on more traditional roles where the man is always in charge and the woman is submissive. In either case, trouble may bubble over when the midlife man tries to master his mounting insecurity by changing his lifestyle.

The fourth male factor is *self-involvement*. The man is crying out for someone—anyone—to see *him*, hear *him*, touch *him*, feel *him*. Everyone likes to be appreciated and desired, but Gratch says that "what greed is to capitalism, narcissism is to personal growth." When a man is self-centered to the detriment of his loved ones, he becomes alienated from them and can rationalize moving on to someone who he thinks will fill his emptiness. Self-involvement also promotes precarious behaviors like the high-risk sports in which many midlife men indulge to try to overcome feelings of inadequacy. That is also why fresh sexual conquests temporarily help a man overcome mounting fears of decay.

Male aggression, or a desire to demonstrate who is in charge at home or at work, is responsible for hypercritical behavior that instigates fights that hurt feelings. Gratch suggests a man's need to prove that he is the boss may be tamed if the partner is able to respond with an offensive that sets limits as to what she will accept, while also showing affection. It's not an easy task with a belligerent—and hurtful—midlife male in her midst.

When a man is unable to express natural aggression toward others, he may turn to another element: *self-destructiveness*. Many men fall into this negative pattern at midlife, thinking of themselves as losers—especially when their self-image is changing, their job security is threatened, and they feel vulnerable physically. This dynamic may lead to the addictions and compulsive syndromes that often destroy marriages. Gratch warns that spouses should never assume responsibility for the man's behavior, which echoes the club members' mantra that it is *his* problem, not *yours*.

The last of Gratch's attributes comes as no surprise to club members: *sexual acting-out*—or "I want sex now." Because men are more quickly aroused, they develop the ability to sexualize their thoughts more easily than women. Gratch says they are more likely to "seek the powerful reward of arousal and orgasm to escape, or cope with, emotional conflicts." In the end many men work out many of their emotional issues—the ones they cannot express verbally—in the sexual arena. Although sex may seem to be the point, ultimately it may not be about sex after all. Gratch demonstrates how all the other male elements play out sexually, with insecurity leading to erectile dysfunction as well as affairs, but he concludes "even that which divides men and women need not be polarizing. With a bit of love and a lot of work even our very opposite can become our best complement."

Even if a midlife crisis does not strike all men, when it does, a woman involved with such a man needs to be prepared. His closest ally may be an understanding wife and a strong marriage. Yet, at this time in his life, he is liable to have neither. His wife may not realize he is struggling—or she may not be sympathetic because of her own problems. He may also find it difficult to explain what he is feeling to her. While he is looking for greater meaning in his humdrum life or trying to explore the depths of his soul, his communication with his wife may center around the daily minutia of managing a busy family. With most wives now working, both spouses are often too tired or busy to make time for romance. Many midlife sexual relationships may be almost nonexistent. A man may find his marriage as boring as his sensible car: It has four wheels and gets him there, but the ride isn't fun anymore. As he begins to ruminate about what could have been or what he wishes he could have, his conflicted signals spark tensions that eventually become unbearable.

Some experts suggest that everyone with midlife issues experiences some degree of unhappiness. For some, this unhappiness itself is *the* major symptom. Fortunately for most people, this time of reckoning is but a transitory stocktaking that does not last. Just as the crisis in an illness is the critical period during which a patient either succumbs or takes a turn toward recovery, the peak of a midlife crisis can lead to a change for the better. If pressures force the man into behaviors that destroy the relationship, the tragic aftermath can haunt him the rest of his life.

Below is a list of consequences that can develop out of a male midlife crisis:

- Alcoholism

- Drug abuse

- Impulsive job changes

- Monetary loss

- Poor investments

- Unhappy marriages

- Affairs

- Domestic violence

- Child abuse

- Family desertion

- Divorce

Alarm Sirens

Since Midlife Wives Club members continue to grapple for clues as to whether a midlife crisis is a passing phase, they have suggested phrases that are red flags for a marriage that is fading. Heather proposed the aggravating response, "I don't know," as in: "Wife: 'What do you want for dinner?' Husband: 'I don't know.' Wife: 'Do you love me?' Husband: 'I don't know.' "

Lee contributed her least favorite dialogue. "Wife: 'Love ya!' Husband: 'Ditto.' What the hell is 'ditto'? Are two words too many to utter in one breath?"

Marlene's husband, Archer, hinted at concerns by saying, "When the boys go to college, I don't want us to look at each other and decide we have nothing in common anymore." The problem was he began saying this when their children were under 12.

Other club members were blindsided by petty issues that became federal cases. Lois said Kevin complained he had the same lunch every day for eight years. "That's true, but usually he made it and would not accept any embellishments I tried to add."

Kristin* had an even more outlandish grievance from her husband. "Dan told our marriage counselor that he couldn't live with me anymore because I serve salad out of a bag!" She said, "Can you imagine telling that to the judge when he asks, 'What are the grounds for divorce?' and your husband responds, 'Bagged salad'?"

Other stock phrases that might trip alarms:

- "We're drifting apart."

- "I don't know what I want."

- "It isn't you."

- "It's not about you; it's about me."

- "I haven't been happy for a long time."

- "I'm feeling (pick one): overwhelmed, smothered, cornered, unhappy, boxed in, ignored." (Then blaming his spouse for making him feel that way.)

- "I feel liked a trapped animal and I need to be free."

- "I would be so much happier with you out of my life." (Or, if he has already left home: "I'm happier now.")

- "I don't miss you at all."

- "The other woman makes me feel like you never did."

- "You deserve someone better than me." (As though he is only looking out for his wife's best interests by leaving.)

Club members are warned that lots of silence could be as worrisome as any of the typical comments. However, the "I love you, but I'm not in love with you anymore" speech brings more tears than any other. If a woman hears that one, club members concur that a crash may be around the next bend.

Midlife crisis might be *ruled out* if:

- He is fooling around and he is 25.

- He is buying a fast car and he is 75.

- He has been unhappy for many years, and everyone knows it.

- There has been no character change—he has always been insensitive and selfish.

- He has been unfaithful other times at other ages.

- He has been mentally or physically abusive for many years.

- He has been chronically dishonest.

- He has had a personality change and he is not in the 40 through 60 age range.

- He has a psychological illness (diagnosed or undiagnosed) such as bipolar disorder.

- He has a (diagnosed or undiagnosed) medical problem.

While these problems may seriously affect a relationship, they do not fit into the midlife crisis model and must be tackled on a case by case basis. Medical and mental health issues require professional help. Abuse cannot be tolerated at any time. Lying and cheating are unlikely to improve with age. Even if the signs are positive for a crisis, most will not permanently ruin a strong marriage. Everyone faces tough situations like a death in the family or financial setbacks. Working together is the best remedy—if he will accept loving assistance. Sometimes waiting it out is the best advice of all. But if all the sirens and whistles are going off, members of the club will offer ways to become a road warrior for a terrifying trip.

CHAPTER 4

Potholes and Bumpy Roads: Stages Along Life's Journey

The long, dull, monotonous years of middle-aged prosperity or middle-aged adversity are excellent campaigning weather for the devil.

—C. S. Lewis, written in 1941, age 43

Even though the Midlife Wives Club members' problems seem unique, they are not. The midlife demographic is huge. Every six seconds somebody in the United States turns 50. At 78 million strong, baby boomers comprise 30 percent of the population.

Since they are the most affluent group, they are also the nation's most lucrative consumers. Marketers know that boomers' midlife crises are real, and have labeled sub-groups "Power Players" and "Fun Seekers." Yet in order to feel powerful and have fun, some of these go-go guys are pushing their vanity forward and setting their families aside. While this attitude might be a boon to luxury car salesmen and plastic surgeons, the middle-aged woman is threatened by the svelte images used to sell her husband everything from cars to condoms.

Profound changes shake most people as they enter their forties and fifties. The 1994 General Social Survey asked a representative sample of Americans whether they had experienced any trauma in the past 12 months. Overall, 40 percent said they had. This proportion was lowest (27 percent) among people in their early thirties, and highest among the middle-aged, rising to 49 percent among people in their late forties and peaking at 53 percent among 50- to 54-year-olds. Invariably, the crises of midlife revolve around the issues that are most important—families, jobs, and personal health.

For boomers in their late forties, their careers may have reached a plateau. Many find it hard to believe they will have to work another two decades before they can consider retiring, a reality felt more keenly when the financial markets showed their fickle nature in recent years. Most boomers say they sometimes or always feel burned out by their jobs or exhausted at the end of the workday. With the giddy days of swift promotion and pay raises behind them, people in their forties no longer see limitless futures and feel trapped. One-third of workers say they would quit if they had enough money to live comfortably for the rest of their lives. The proportion rises to 42 percent among 45- to 49-year-olds and peaks among 55- to 59-year-olds at 50 percent.

"I could graph Stefan's moods with the ups and downs of the stock market," Elinor said. "He thought he had invested his retirement funds brilliantly and was planning to retire early, but the worse the economy got, the more trapped he felt. Now his parents need more nursing care, and he's fretting about having to cover their shortfall in a few years."

This sandwich generation—who may be responsible for both children and aging parents—may feel imprisoned by duty. The percentage of Americans—both male and female—who say their life is stimulating drops below 50 percent among those in their forties. Those who believe that extramarital sex is always wrong falls below 70 percent among people in their forties—the lowest level among all groups except the youngest ages 18 to 24. Interestingly, the proportion of Americans who admit to ever having an extramarital affair peaks in the 45 to 49 age group at 22 percent.

Divorce is another direction baby boom women may take far faster than earlier generations. Instead of putting up with their husbands' wandering eyes, these wage earners feel more secure about striking out on their own. Demographers expect a surge in midlife divorce as fed-up women, who have long worked a second shift at home, finally close the door on their misbehaving men.

Lee faced a turning point when she realized she could survive without James. "The bottom line for me is our son. He's very confused and we can't live in limbo forever. Either James decides to be part of the family or he doesn't. I can't save this marriage on my own."

Bad Boy or Midlife Rebel?

Many women ask whether their husbands are just being naughty or are truly troubled. Often they feel that their mates are acting out of a selfish need to have their cake and eat it too rather than struggling with deep psychological issues. "When a guy knows exactly what he wants and goes for it no matter who is in the way and is happy with his decision even though he had to break up his family to get to where he wanted to be, he's rebelling," Zoë declared. "On the other hand, midlife crisis is when he leaves his family hoping to find happiness—and after all the commotion, he still does not find peace or contentment."

Bonnie thought that the crisis is a crucible where a man's mettle is tested. "If he walks away from family, friends, his whole way of life, to embrace something so totally out of character that it leaves everyone shaking their heads, then he has failed. If he weathers the storm and makes adjustments—without throwing away everything—then he's passed through the fire and becomes stronger like iron forged into steel. Unfortunately, Nigel failed miserably, and what he did to our family was unforgivable."

Psychology 101

From earliest times philosophers, spiritual leaders, and psychologists have tried to find an order to behavior and its implications in the meaning of life. Most modern assumptions on the psychological dynamics of life cycles began when Carl Jung disagreed with some of Sigmund Freud's theories. Freud believed that a person's adjustment to adulthood was determined by his childhood influences, while Jung reasoned that the psyche matured from the cradle to the grave. Jung stated, "If everything goes back to childhood, then everything is someone's fault and trust in the power of taking responsibility for oneself is determined." Comparing life cycles to the sun's cycle, he divided a person's life into two major periods—morning and afternoon—then broke them down further into childhood, early maturity, middle age, and late maturity.

Jung was especially fascinated with middle age and popularized the phenomenon of midlife crisis, which he suggested happened to men around age 40, but to women somewhat earlier. He surmised that people entered midlife thinking that the skills that had served them during the first half of life would be applicable to the second half. But they are not. The transition period—or crisis—is the process during which everyone must reevaluate all aspects of their lives. If we are able to relinquish our self-centered attitudes about what is best for us and develop a deeper concern for others, we may find the true meaning of life. Otherwise we may decline into despair.

Jung proposed there should be a crisis during each stage of human development and this crisis is merely a task that needs to be mastered. He explained, "Crisis is used here in a developmental sense to connote not a threat of catastrophe, but a turning point." Thus each crisis can be seen as a fork in the road that leads a person down the next path of human development, and each choice leads to the formation of the adult personality.

His Turn: Stan

"Every day seems to be a different shade of the same gray haze, no matter whether the sun is shining or not. I hate the anxiety, panic attacks, and feelings of impending doom. By now I thought I would be so much farther along life's path. I hate the analogy of the afternoon of one's life. I'd like to ring Carl Jung's neck. Where did my dreams go? I need to change something; I just don't know what or why. So I just sit here staring at my keyboard. It reads: 'CTRL-ALT-DEL.'

"CTRL: If I control my feelings, it leads to more heartache. ALT: If I found an alternate woman and established a relationship, would that make me feel better? Probably. For about an hour. DEL: Delete my marriage? That's what'd happen if I ALT'd! In fact, I'd probably be shot to death. Wait. Maybe that is the way out of this mess after all. Hell, I don't know anymore. I know there's a light somewhere at the end of the tunnel; I just hope it doesn't burn out before I reach it."

Erik H. Erikson combined some of both Jung's and Freud's theories to demonstrate that the ego is shaped by psychological as well as biological forces. Erikson's eight stages of development from birth to old age have direct implications for why some people have more severe midlife crises than others. If a person successfully resolves the task for each stage, he will tend to have fewer problems with adjustments later in life. If a problem remains unresolved, there may be direct consequences during the midlife reevaluation.

Erikson's Stages of Human Development

Age: *Infancy—0 to 1*

Stage: *Trust versus Mistrust*

Task: *Establish trusting relationships*

Trust (or emotional attachment) is established when babies are given adequate warmth, touching, love, and physical attention. *Mistrust* is caused by inadequate or unpredictable care by parents who are cold, indifferent, or rejecting. People who do not adequately attach during this period may have long-term difficulties in forming and keeping relationships.

Midlife consequences: Marital problems sometimes can be traced to inconsistencies or upheavals that led a child to *distrust* his caregivers.

Age: *Toddler—1 to 2*

Stage: *Autonomy versus Shame and Doubt*

Task: *Learning to separate from parents*

Children express growing self-control by climbing, touching, exploring, and gaining a desire to do more for themselves. *Autonomy* is fostered by encouraging children to try new skills. *Shame* and *doubt* result from parents who ridicule, overprotect, or discipline harshly.

Midlife consequences: Children who suffered much *shame* may *doubt* their abilities. Their low self-esteem may become a renewed burden in middle age.

Age: *Early Childhood—2 to 6*

Stage: *Initiative versus Guilt*

Task: *Safely venturing on their own*

The child moves from simple self-control to an ability to take *initiative*. The child learns to plan, undertake, and carry out tasks through play. Pretending helps children practice more mature social skills and roles. *Initiative* is gained when parents allow the child independence to ask questions, use imagination, and to choose pursuits.

Midlife consequences: Children who were made to feel *guilty* about the activities they instigated by being severely criticized, not being allowed to play, having questions discouraged, or being overprotected during this phase may search for more freedom again at midlife.

Age: *Primary and Middle School—6 to 12*

Stage: *Industry versus Inferiority*

Task: *Learning to feel self-confident*

During the elementary school years, children develop a positive sense of *industry* if they are praised for and feel successful at building, painting, cooking, reading, studying, and other productive activities. Feelings of *inferiority* result when the child is unable to accomplish these tasks or is regarded as messy, childish, or inadequate.

Midlife consequences: If feelings of *inferiority* overwhelm a man at work or at home, he may try to overcome them with a new job—or woman.

Age: *Adolescence—12 to 18*

Stage: *Identity versus Role Confusion*

Task: *Answering the question "Who am I?"*

The adolescent must build a consistent *identity* out of self-perceptions and relationships with others. If unsuccessful, the adolescent will sink into *role confusion*, unable to make decisions and choices, especially about vocation, sexual orientation, and his role in life in general.

Midlife consequences: If this step is incomplete, a second rebellion to establish a new *role* in midlife may occur.

Age: *Young Adulthood—18 to 40*

Stage: *Intimacy versus Isolation*

Task: *Share meaningful love or deep friendships with others*

Intimacy means an ability to care about others and to share experiences with them. Many adult relationships remain superficial and unfulfilling. Failure to establish *intimacy* leads to a deep sense of *isolation*. Other activities may be substituted for *intimacy*: sex, success, work, money, hobbies, children.

Midlife consequences: If a person feels *isolated* at midlife, he may look for new ways to find the *intimacy* he craves.

Age: *Middle Adulthood—40 to 65*

Stage: *Generativity versus Self-absorption and Stagnation*

Task: *Caring about oneself, one's children, and the future*

Generativity is achieved by guiding one's own children, by help-ing other children (for instance as a teacher, clergyman, or coach), or through productive or creative work. A person's con-cern and energies must be less self-centered and broadened to include the welfare of others and of society as a whole. One becomes *stagnant* when life loses meaning and the person feels bitter, lifeless, and trapped.

Midlife consequences: The sense of *stagnation* is the crux of midlife crisis.

Age: *Late Adulthood—65 to death*

Stage: *Integrity versus Despair*

Task: *Reviewing one's past with acceptance and satisfaction*

Integrity results from having lived richly and responsibly. This allows a person to face aging and death with dignity. *Despair* comes if previous life events are surveyed with regret.

Midlife consequences: If there is a sense that life has been a series of missed opportunities, that one has failed, and it is too late to reverse what has been done, aging and the threat of death become a source of fear, *despair*, and depression.

Everyone—male and female—must pass through each stage. No task can be skipped and nobody is immune. We meet each challenge based on our genetic tendencies, family, and societal environment, as well as the luck of the draw. A man may not have meant to marry young, but if his girlfriend was pregnant, he may have made that decision and then has to pay the psychic cost at midlife when he has to revisit and complete some of the issues around identity versus role confusion. Or perhaps intimacy was always a problem but it finally ate away at him when he realizes his marriage is not offering him the satisfaction for which he yearns. Club members often report how problems growing up or in early adulthood precipitated midlife crisis during the seventh stage.

"For years I kept trying to get Rudy to tell me what was bothering him, but he kept everything bottled inside," Jasmine explained. "In his family expressing emotions was forbidden. Now he can't wait to share his feelings with everyone—except me!"

According to Erikson, if everything goes right, there is a virtuous payoff in each of the stages. A well-nurtured infant develops a sense of hope. Someone who has weathered the tribulations of being a teen learns fidelity. If a young adult overcomes isolation, he is able to establish an intimate relationship with a partner and is rewarded by feelings of mutual love. If the midlife person is able to give back to his own family as well as society in general, caring is the virtue of his successful evolution. However, a man who becomes preoccupied with his hair or muscle loss or who obsesses over fast cars and sexy women may be too caught up in self-absorption to make progress in terms of leaving something valuable to the next generation—whether through parenting or a work of art, music, or even a financial bequest.

When Gay and her husband Philip's son graduated college

and another son was in his second year, they found themselves struggling with a jumble of lonely feelings. Grandchildren seemed eons away and a pall of sadness colored what should have been a relaxing vacation when they admitted they missed sharing many of the activities with a young person. A few days after returning home, they signed up for foster care and adoption classes. Looking around the room, Gay noticed that more than half the class was older than 40 and realized that many in the group had a strong desire to give back to needy youth. When they adopted a 12-year-old girl, Gay and Philip discovered that parenting a middle-school child, who needed car pooling, braces, and help with science projects, made stagnation impossible.

Gail Sheehy, author of both *Passages* and *Understanding Men's Passages*, breaks the second half of life into three general periods including provisional adulthood (18 to 30), first adulthood (30 to 45), and second adulthood (45 to 85+), which is further divided into the age of mastery (45 to 65) and the age of integrity (65 to 85+). Sheehy also describes several additional phases including the "flourishing forties," the "fearless fifties," and the "influential sixties." Although Sheehy points out the trials and tribulations that men face at each milestone, she avoids negative life scripts. Her men of 40 have opportunities to redefine themselves as fathers, spouses, and providers. At 50 they can take charge of their destiny by calling more of the shots about their own lives and actively recoup what they think they may have lost. Men of 60 may choose not to retire or find ways to make their lives more meaningful. Sheehy points out the wealth of opportunities for men to elect generativity over stagnation, integrity over despair.

To Sheehy, the decade between 45 and 55 is often a "bonus stage" during which people can reevaluate where they have been and map where they will go next. They can decide if they want to take the same passengers or offer new ones a berth. They can plot new adventures, try on new personas, rid themselves of disliked labels, follow a new spiritual path, learn a fresh skill, make healthier lifestyle changes to increase longevity, as well as decide what to leave as a legacy.

Middle of the Road

Just as bored children whine "How much longer?" during interminable car rides, the midlife man doesn't review how far he has come but wonders "How much time do I have left?" The germ of generativity may be related to a need for immortality. A book on a library shelf, a group of tutored students, an invention—all are concrete reminders that he may have made a difference. The problem is that unless a man has had a safe voyage through the turbulent seas of each prior stage, he may not get to shore with enough cargo to distribute to others.

Lorraine was on the receiving end of Walt's rebellion. "In five months he has ruined our lives on all fronts: financial, emotional, security, friendship, trust, and health. He has destroyed my spirit, my soul, my confidence. Then Walt has the gall to tell me that although it was harder than he thought to leave me and our family, living with her is more beautiful than he expected. How can you build love on a foundation of someone else's despair?"

Sadly, stagnation not only destroys the true meaning of life, which is to leave something good behind, but it also harms those who expected to be protected and nurtured. If a self-absorbed midlife man has to annihilate his family to "find himself," he not only wounds his child when he leaves, but also passes on a tragic inheritance because successful passage through whatever stage his child is in is thwarted, which may result in negative consequences in subsequent stages of that young person's life.

His Turn: Ellis

"It's been said that change is the one constant in the universe. We live with changes, and adapt to them, throughout our lives. Typically, there is some level of reasoning behind the changes we encounter. Midlife crisis, on the other hand, defies reasoning. Personal fulfillment becomes more important than family happiness. Core values fall by the wayside and suddenly adultery or abandoning your family appear to be acceptable behaviors. Lifelong religious beliefs are set aside. Lying—or lies of omission—become easier. And the worst thing is that no amount of logic sways the thinking of the person mired in this tar pit."

Daniel J. Levinson is perhaps the best-known chronicler of men's changes between 35 and 45. At Yale in the late 1960s, Levinson undertook a five-year multidisciplinary study funded by the National Institute of Mental Health that led to his book *The Seasons of a Man's Life.* He also believed that adult development never ceases. Each man is influenced by his sociocultural milieu (ethnicity, religion, class, political system, family, profession); his unconscious and subconscious wishes, conflicts, and worries; as well as the way he participates in society. Levinson interviewed only 40 men—ten each who were biologists, novelists, executives, and blue-collar workers—and found that around 80 percent did experience a crisis at midlife. For these men crisis did not mean a mere change or transition, but an acute predicament. "Because a man in this crisis is often somewhat irrational, others may regard him as 'upset' or 'sick.' In most cases, he is not. The man himself and those who care about him should recognize that he is in a normal developmental period and is working on normal midlife tasks. The desire to question and modify his life stems from the most healthy part of the self." Levinson says that while reappraisal is appropriate, problems arise when baggage carried from hard times in the past may block change. As Midlife Wives Club members know, this reappraisal is not merely a private intellectual process because many men feel compelled to explore the limits, find out how it feels to be with another woman, or try out another job, hobby, or lifestyle. All the while he is fulfilling three tasks: finishing up any old business left over from early childhood by reappraising the choices he has made, taking steps to create a fresh structure for middle adulthood, and completing the individuation process—all which change the person's relationship to himself and the world.

Theologians like Paul Tillich suggest that religious salvation is closely connected to psychological healing. If psychologists have pinpointed the crux of the midlife terror as fear of death and if generativity and integrity are the antidotes, then eternal salvation prevents self-destruction and annihilation. The natural upheavals at midlife force men to confront their mortality as well as question their prior spiritual assumptions. In midlife a man may return to his religious roots or change to a place of worship that is more in tune with the beliefs he has garnered through life experience and where he feels a stronger sense of community.

Lauren was active in church her whole life, but Nick didn't start to attend services until they met. "He admired my 'inner peace' and soon we regularly went to my church until his midlife crisis two years ago. Then Nick started questioning if there is a God and didn't want to worship in public any longer."

For a while Lauren avoided Sunday services because she didn't know what to say when the older ladies asked, "Where's that handsome guy of yours today?" Lauren said her faith has not wavered. "If anything, I pray more than ever because I need God's strength to get through this."

A spiritual renewal may be what is needed to overcome stagnation. This can take many forms, from a reaffirmation of faith to accepting a new one to being open to divine intervention. The goal is to move from the self-centeredness of "the man who dies with the most toys wins" to a genuine caring for others—family, friends, community, posterity, God.

His Turn: Dusty

"My wife started attending a different church than the one in which I was raised. At first I attended services with her, but as I became more uncomfortable with the preaching, she became more insistent that I join. So I backed away altogether and soon after that we separated. My faith was weak, and although I never quit believing in God, I continued to ask forgiveness for my sins.

"After we divorced, I searched for a church of my own—not the one of my parents or my ex-wife. Finally, I am at peace with God. My midlife crisis was a near-death experience, and I found rebirth in my renewed spirituality and religion."

No Outlet: Why Some Men Run Away

Why do sensible men who were good providers suddenly straddle crotch rockets and leave a tearful family in the dust? According to an African fable, every morning the gazelle wakes up. It knows that it must outrun the lion or it will be killed. Every morning a lion wakes up and knows that it must catch a gazelle or it will starve. When the sun comes up, it doesn't matter if you are a lion or a gazelle, you had better be running. The midlife man feels he must be the predator or he will be the prey. Overwhelmed, the fight-or-flight response takes over.

His Turn: Chuck

"I'm 45, have been married 19 years, and have three children. From the outside we have the perfect life: no financial worries and everything we need. But something is missing. Life is a grind. I hate being away from home 11 hours a day, then after fighting traffic, coming home to fighting kids and an exhausted wife.

"I have to put my wishes aside to car pool for sports and spend weekends with the family or catch up on house and yard work. I don't have any time for myself now and don't anticipate any of this changing for at least a decade. By then I'll be in my mid-fifties. I'm not about to buy a sports car or go looking for another woman—even though my marriage could use some spice—but I feel like I'm searching for something, although I don't have a clue what."

Harvard physiologist Walter Cannon conducted experiments that established the basis for the "fight-or-flight" description of stress in 1920. Cannon found that reactions to a threat followed the same physiological patterns, though varying in degree depending on the risk of the situation. In 1936 Hans Selye discovered that changes in the state of human organs were the same despite the source of the stress induced on the human body. He described the general adaptation syndrome, which consists of three stages. *Alarm*, which happens instantaneously, unites the body's resources to battle the stressor and opens the door for the fight-or-flight response. Next comes *resistance*, which forces the body to combat the stressor—a car veering toward us, a summons to the principal's office, a reaction to a bee sting. *Exhaustion* follows if equilibrium does not return. So if physical activity or talking about the problem—two classic ways of "letting off steam"—don't work, pent up fear, anger, or frustration may find an outlet in either emotional or physical illness.

The fight-or-flight response is controlled by the sympathetic and parasympathetic nervous systems. The sympathetic nervous system prepares the body for action and makes energy resources available to the body. It is galvanized when we focus on external trials such as completing a challenging task. This is also the system that is fueled by adrenaline in a stressful situation—whether induced by a rollercoaster ride or hearing frightening news. The more cataclysmic the event, the more the sympathetic nervous system is taxed to its maximum capacity.

Switching off the fear component and assuming the "fight" mode is what spurs men to be able to go to war, scale mountains, test supersonic airplanes, bungy jump, or start up new companies. Nevertheless, a healthy dose of fear is protective and prevents pushing the pedal to the floor, skydiving without a reserve chute, and risking all of one's savings in the stock market. Throughout life, managing stress is a balancing act between what must be accomplished, outside pressures, and internal compulsions. At midlife the fulcrum is wobbling and equilibrium must once again be established.

In order to slog it out in the competitive world—be it the boardroom or the highway—we are trained to keep anxieties at bay, but this has consequences. Many people's frustrations are coiled like a toy snake in a trickster's can—witness road rage, spouse abuse, and other anger management issues.

His Turn: Stan

"I've been thinking about how to talk to my wife about this monster before it gets too far gone. I want her to know that I'm having troubles, but I haven't been able to think of a good way to break the ice. I'm scared and I feel like hell and I don't know why. I wish I was 20 years younger so I could live my life again and not screw it up like I have. For years I've numbed my feelings, and the penalty is that I've felt emotionally absent from my family. Now I think I'm falling in love with a potential other woman. Maybe there's time to work something out with my wife before I do something I will regret."

Just as fear and anxiety trigger biochemical changes that lead to fight or flight, falling in love activates a similar hormonal rush. The brain's hypothalamus releases phenylethylamine or PEA, an amphetamine-like substance that is mildly hallucinogenic. Also produced is dopamine, which is a motivator and activates a sense of well-being, and norepinephrine, a neurotransmitter that produces a rapid heartbeat, dilated pupils, and sweaty palms. Physiologically, falling in love is not too different from falling off a cliff; it is the same fight-or-flight response. And it is deliciously addictive. The person daydreams about his new love interest, he becomes obsessed with e-mail and voice mail, he sneaks out to call her, and he experiences a further frisson of excitement hiding it all from his wife—as there once was when he defied his mother's curfews or broke high school rules.

Unfortunately, the chemical high of romance cannot be sustained indefinitely. Anthropologist Helen Fisher suggests the buzz wears off in an average of 18 months to three years, which is why many marriages fail in the first few years and also why running off with another woman rarely brings real peace or happiness to the midlife male.

Midlife may be the last chance to get it right. During the crisis a man grapples with the issues of young versus old, destruction versus creation, masculine versus feminine, and attachment versus separateness. In middle adulthood the most crucial seems to be the young/old schism that turns an optimist into a pessimist seeing his glass of life as half-empty. The balding man who has recently lost a parent or friend and may be having physical problems is clobbered by the reality of his own mortality. Many of the Midlife Wives Club members' spouses attempt to deny signs of aging by driving faster, running from responsibility, or taking up with younger women who—unlike their wives—do not remind them of their mothers. A man brought up to bottle his emotions and who had a distant father may not be in touch with his more feminine, nurturing side. In midlife he may not need to be as competitive in work, may find joy cuddling with his grandchildren, and thus may be able to reconcile the masculine/feminine polarity in a way that is more emotionally satisfying either by becoming closer to his family or finding someone else to gratify that need. Even though old age is decades away, the midlife man often fears death more than any other time in his life. But if he can come to grips with his dread, he can develop creative strategies for a more meaningful life as well as bequeathing a legacy. If not, he may make a series of destructive choices that tear apart his family and undermine his future.

CHAPTER 5

Signposts to Hell:
Facing Serious Issues

Chaos of thought and passion, all confused;
Still by himself abused or disabused;
Created half to rise, and half to fall;
Great lord of all things, yet prey to all;
Sole judge of truth, in endless error hurled;
The glory, jest, and riddle of the world.

—Alexander Pope, written in 1733, age 45

Midlife Wives Club members grapple with the chicken-and-egg conundrum. What comes first: their husband's midlife crisis or his depression? Lois said that Kevin was depressed for several years but would never admit it. "Maybe if he had worked on that, the crisis would never have happened, and he could have coped better with his father's death."

Lee said her husband had the same problems, but in reverse order. "James' depression was prompted by grief for his father, and midlife crisis followed after that."

"Rory was in fine spirits," remarked Colleen, "until the other woman left the country—although I didn't know this at the time. So he was having his midlife crisis before she left, and the depression came on after." However, it was the depression that clued Colleen that something was going on.

"Depression triggered Fred's crisis," reported Polly. "When he felt gloomy, he hated his whole life." Polly agreed that they needed to make changes, "but the depression made him so desperate that our life turned into an unhappy, unhealthy calamity."

Depression Detours

Not only is depression frequently bundled with midlife crisis, it also may be what propels a man into a crisis. In the case of the husband, it often activates his fight-or-flight reflex, and some experts believe reawakened adolescent despair and unresolved sexual issues are some of the root causes. When the midlife male becomes dissatisfied with himself, he may brood for hours. Self-pity and self-criticism gnaw at his self-confidence. As he turns his anger inward, depression may rise to the surface. Reserves that helped him manage previous low points in his life may be depleted. And, if unchecked, depression can lead to other, more serious consequences for himself and his family.

"Depression kicked off Robert's change," Evie recalled. "He saw his whole life and our marriage in a negative light, which made him desperate to get away, try something new, anything to make him feel differently."

Just as women in menopause are at higher risk for depression due to the hormonal changes, the male chemical counterpart also has been indicted. Between ages 40 and 60, approximately 40 percent of men will experience lethargy, depression, increased irritability, mood swings, and some degree of difficulty in attaining and sustaining erections. However, male depression often goes unrecognized because men don't always present classic symptoms. Men may deny erectile dysfunction or ignore more subtle changes, but depression can be life-threatening. Men commit 80 percent of all suicides, and the rate at midlife is three times higher and increases to seven times higher at age 65. Although depression awareness has come a long way in recent years—especially with the mass-marketing of antidepressant medications—studies indicate that it may take up to ten years and three health professionals for depression to be properly diagnosed. Fortunately, of those who do get help, more than 80 percent find relief.

His Turn: Stan

"I am miserable, but I am afraid to seek counseling because this is a small town and I'd feel ashamed if I ran into my therapist on the street. But if I go to a counselor, it will be a female because I'd be more embarrassed to cry in front of a man.

"I also read everything I can find on the Internet, most of which doesn't apply to me—but sends me back to that blue area. Maybe I'm still in denial about this problem."

Polly pointed out how many typical signs of midlife crisis also sound like signs of depression. "Even the fast car and young girlfriend are often attempts to self-medicate or mask depression because they make a man feel better, at least for a short while."

Combine frustration and insecurity with a general sense of the uselessness of life and you have a midlife male drowning in a sea of helplessness. These feelings tend to become self-feeding. The more powerless he feels, the more impotent he becomes. The more impotent he becomes, the more evident his inadequate feelings. While many men facing midlife crisis do not automatically become depressed, they should watch out for the major symptoms, and if they believe that at least five have been present almost every day for a two-week period, and also represent a change from their previous function, they should seek medical advice. Only a physician can prescribe medication, although other therapists such as psychologists and clinical social workers can refer a client for medical treatment.

Below is a list of symptoms of depression:

- Feeling irritable most of the day

- A diminished interest or no pleasure in all, or almost all, activities most of the day

- Significant weight loss when not dieting, or weight gain, or decrease or increase in appetite

- Moving or speaking so slowly that other people notice

- Moving around or being more restless than usual

- Insomnia or sleeping excessively

- Being more active or much less physically active than usual

- Fatigue or loss of energy

- Feelings of worthlessness or excessive or inappropriate guilt

- Diminished ability to think or concentrate, or indecisiveness

- Thoughts of being better off dead or wanting to hurt oneself

- Recurrent thoughts of suicide, with or without a specific plan

According to endocrinologist Adrian Dobs of the Johns Hopkins School of Medicine in Baltimore, diminished testosterone levels play a part in male midlife change, but this does not tell the whole story. Other hormones change as well, including pituitary, growth hormones, and another called DHEA, although these fluctuations don't necessarily occur at the same time. There are also psychosocial adjustments, such as the way a couple relates to each other after the children leave home or when a woman goes back to work. "It's a big, complex picture," says Dr. Harvey Sternbach of UCLA. "You have to look at everything that's going on in a man's life." Nevertheless, there is a connection between low testosterone and depression. One study of 850 men over age 50 showed the lower the hormone levels, the higher their scores on a depression test. A much smaller study of depressed men indicated those men who didn't feel better on antidepressants alone improved after testosterone supplements were included in their regimen.

In recent years, depression has been considered psychiatry's most treatable condition. Even so, fewer than one in five seek professional help, and most of those are women. By directing their pain outward, many depressed men hurt the people they love.

His Turn: Adam

"Two months ago I too was flirting with the idea of meeting the woman I found online. Even though I thought I was going crazy, I did not lose my sanity, and I have not acted on my feelings. The hardest step was telling my wife about how uncertain I felt about the future looming like a sucking void. My wife amazed me with how receptive she has been. Maybe that's because I didn't blame her for my problems. I said, 'I feel this way about myself' and 'I need you to help me deal with these issues.' But I couldn't tell her everything or she would have been hurt. So that is where my therapist really helped."

His Depression versus Her Depression

Men and women experience depression differently. Women tend to use food, friends, and love to self-medicate, while men turn to alcohol, TV, sports, and sex. While women often say their problems could be solved if they could be a better spouse, co-worker, parent, or friend, men believe their problems could be solved only if their spouse, co-worker, parent, or friend would treat them better. Women constantly wonder, "Am I lovable enough?" while their men worry, "Am I being loved enough?" Other differences include:

DEPRESSED WOMAN	DEPRESSED MAN
Blames herself	Feels others are to blame
Feels sad, apathetic, and worthless	Feels angry, irritable, and has inflated ego
Feels anxious and scared	Feels suspicious and guarded
Avoids conflicts at all costs	Creates conflicts
Always tries to be nice	Acts overtly or covertly hostile
Withdraws when feeling hurt	Attacks when feeling hurt
Has trouble with self-respect	Demands respect from others
Feels she was born to fail	Feels the world set him up to fail
Feels lethargic and nervous	Feels restless and agitated
Becomes a chronic procrastinator	Becomes a compulsive time keeper
Sleeps too much	Sleeps too little
Has trouble setting boundaries	Needs control at all costs

Feels guilty for what she does	Feels ashamed for who he is
Is uncomfortable receiving praise	Is frustrated if not praised enough
Finds it easy to talk about weaknesses and doubts	Is terrified to talk about weaknesses and doubts
Has a strong fear of success	Has a strong fear of failure
Needs to "blend in" to feel safe	Needs to be "top dog" to feel safe

Lee said James refused to consider medications for depression because "if he could not fix himself no one else could fix him." Though James was unwilling to take medication while they were together, his doctor did put him on an antidepressant after the separation. "At least they helped him realize that he had a son who needed him."

His Turn: Karl

"I credit an antidepressant with freeing me from my downward spiral. I struggled for almost six months, thinking I could beat it, but getting progressively worse. Once I started taking medication, my midlife madness started fading fast. If I had known a year ago today that I could feel so well by popping a few pills, I would have saved myself a journey to hell and back—not to mention the grief I caused my family—before I took control of myself. I'm lucky I didn't go with the urge to trash my whole life. We all need help sometime; we can't always do it on our own."

Depression responds well to a combination of approaches including individual and group psychotherapy, medications, diet and exercise, new or renewed spiritual awareness, new or renewed social supports, and learning self-love and acceptance.

Who's Behind the Wheel?
Four Types of Midlife Men

Researchers Michael P. Farrell and Stanley D. Rosenberg, who worked with some of Daniel J. Levinson's associates at Yale, compared 300 men entering middle age to 150 men in their late twenties and used a variety of tests to measure various aspects of their behavior, attitude, and defenses as well as their mental and physical health. Their work, *Men at Midlife*, identifies four general groups of men:

- Anti-hero

- Punitive-disenchanted

- Pseudo-developed

- Transcendent-generative

The smallest sample, at about 12 percent of the group, was the *anti-heroes*, who were considered in crisis because they were dissatisfied, stressed, and alienated. (Sound familiar?) These were the men who verbalized regrets about their past and yearned to get a fresh start—especially in the workplace. For many, family relations were satisfactory, but others felt suffocated by their wider social milieu. Like many of the male Midlife Wives Club members, these men admitted self-doubt. They also tended to be free of bigotry, but did display psychosomatic symptoms. In movies Woody Allen often portrays the anti-hero type. Other modern classic anti-hero characters include Philip Roth's Portnoy (*Portnoy's Complaint*) and John Updike's Harry Rabbit.

The most seriously dissatisfied group—the *punitive-disenchanted*—comprised 30 percent of the types. These mainly working-class men denied stress, and were the most likely to be depressed and alienated, as well as to have problems with both work and family relationships. Severely in crisis, these men blamed everyone around them—social circle, employers, family, and society—for their hard luck. The punitive-disenchanted men were the most prejudiced and had the worst prognosis for finding happiness because of their lack of introspection. Many resembled the Archie Bunker stereotype.

Another group—the *pseudo-developed* men—constituted 26 percent of the sample. No matter the economic class, they desperately tried to appear to "have it all" to the outside world. They denied problems at home or work and professed high levels of mental and physical well-being. However, psychological tests revealed a high degree of self-deception, inflexible personalities, and hidden narrow-mindedness. These men displaced the anger from within to without. In the movie *Ordinary People*, Donald Sutherland's portrayal of Calvin, the reserved father, epitomizes the pseudo-developed type, as does the surly surgeon Dr. Robert Romano on *ER*.

On the bright side, the largest number of men—over 32 percent—in the four quadrants fell into the *transcendent-generative* category. While admitting that stress did impact their lives, they still were the most satisfied at work and with their families. They also were the most free from anxiety and stress-related symptoms. They were the least prejudiced, most self-possessed, and most able to handle life's ups and downs with equanimity. These men did not seem to have suffered an overt midlife crisis; rather they managed to steer through each obstacle with increasing self-mastery and maturity. Often from the upper echelon of society, transcendent-generative men have the highest levels of education and income. Bill Cosby's warm, fatherly, funny, wise persona embodies this male image, as does former U.S. president Jimmy Carter, who acts as an elder statesman and generative man with his peacemaking and Habitat for Humanity projects.

While the researchers found that the burdens of middle age mounted at about the same pace, the types demonstrated differences in how they reacted to their spouses. Some denied stress, some openly confronted their issues, and some were either satisfied or dissatisfied with their lot in life. Those men openly confronting stress were the anti-hero and transcendent-generative types; those who denied stress were the pseudo-developed and the punitive-disenchanted types.

Fortunately most men move through the midlife period without overt difficulty. However, major depressive illness occurs in about one percent of elderly men, whereas minor depression, or what doctors call "subsyndromal depression," affects 13 to 27 percent of older men, and this can be masked by a variety of unhealthy behaviors, most commonly substance abuse and domestic violence. As we have seen from Midlife Wives Club members who slowly came to understand their mates were entering an acute transition, men start out with vague complaints that do not fit easily into neat boxes. According to an article in *American Family Physician* in 2000, doctors need to be alert for signs of common psychosocial disorders in male patients, especially alcohol and substance abuse, domestic violence, midlife crisis, and depression.

Katie revealed her experiences with a depressed midlife spouse. "Depression can lead to addictive behaviors because they look for something to alleviate their pain." Katie believed that Jeff bounced between relationships and substance abuse. "When nothing from booze to babes cured the underlying cause, his depression deepened, which intensified his midlife woes. It was a vicious circle."

Dr. William A. Nolen exposed his own midlife slide in *Crisis Time: Love, Marriage and the Male at Midlife*. "The male midlife crisis may include all the symptoms of a depression, but there is almost always a major distinguishing feature," he wrote. "The man in depression gives up. He gets so down on himself that he surrenders. He is convinced he is no good and that nothing can be done about it. The man in midlife crisis, however, no matter how down on himself he may be, comes fighting back. He dyes his hair; buys a sports car; starts an affair; raises hell in bars; argues with the boss; makes passes at his friends' wives; quits his job. In short, he does all those things that may get him into serious trouble. The man in depression simply lies on his bed of pain and bemoans his fate. Admittedly, before the man in crisis starts to fight back, his condition may be almost indistinguishable from a depression. So what? When it hits the victim, he doesn't care what it's called. All he wants is to get better. That was my goal."

Nolen is an example of the pseudo-developed type. From the exterior he had everything: a prestigious job and lifestyle, a lovely home and wife, and high-achieving children. But shortly after a successful heart operation, Nolen self-medicated his anxieties, depression, and insomnia with excess drinking and disastrous doses of Valium and quaaludes. Living in a small town in the early 1980s, he was under tremendous stress due to workloads, financial responsibilities, and keeping up appearances. He thought he had nowhere to turn and didn't confide in his wife or friends. Around his fiftieth birthday, he plummeted into a pit of despair. In order to keep going, he was taking almost lethal doses of drugs and alcohol. Finally he admitted to his wife that he could not continue on the same path, and she agreed that he was making everyone's life miserable, not just his own.

The turning point came when he called his doctor and admitted he needed help.

According to Farrell and Rosenberg, if this category of midlife men is compared to their integrated counterparts, they will have more trouble with insomnia (12 percent versus 2 percent) and have ill health affect their work (14 percent versus 7 percent). Although they are not as likely to report drinking excessively, they may be in denial about their usage.

Midlife Depression and Alcohol

Alcohol remains the most heavily consumed drug in America. The highest rates of alcohol abuse are in men 25 to 39 years of age, although alcoholism is also a considerable problem after age 65. Alcohol addiction is considered a depressive equivalent that is measured by the length, amount, and pattern of drinking (steady versus episodic), the social problems that result (divorce, loss of job, traffic violations, arrests), signs of psychological dependency (loss of control, preoccupation), physiological dependence symptoms (tolerance to high blood alcohol levels, withdrawal syndrome, hallucinations, tremors, delirium tremens seizures), and medical complications (liver damage, gastrointestinal bleeding). Middle-aged alcoholics fall into two categories: those who have a history of drinking often dating back to adolescence and those who drink more seriously around their forties in response to depression, loneliness, stress, illness, or some other loss or trauma.

LaVonne's husband, Billy, showed many traits of the antihero type who was wrestling with feelings of alienation as he approached a midlife crisis. His job as a printer had become computerized, and he lacked the skills of the younger employees in this area. Like 39 percent of men in this category, Billy admitted that he drank too much some of the time. LaVonne noticed his drinking patterns had changed. "In the past, Billy might have a few beers after work and enjoyed partying on the weekends, but it never interfered with his life or our marriage. In his mid-forties, I noticed he'd go straight to the fridge for a beer the minute he got home from work, then wouldn't stop drinking until he fell asleep watching TV." LaVonne didn't want to make a big deal about it because she thought he needed to relax. Later, though, the symptoms started to mount, and LaVonne began to worry that the excess drinking was a cover-up for deeper problems. "What bothered me most was that his interest in sex decreased to almost nothing."

Jasmine said that Rudy became upset when their daughter sent in her college applications around the time he was reviewing his retirement options. "He's talking about becoming a mentor or even teaching an evening course in his field." Rudy fit the transcendent-generative model in that he seemed satisfied with his work and family. While he still had to cope with developmental issues as he examined his life and planned the next phase, he was more likely to have a transition than a crisis. Even so, Rudy drank almost daily with business associates, had a cocktail before dinner at home, and wine as well. He was in the at-risk category for alcoholism and he promised his wife that he would cut back. "I know he shouldn't drink so much, but I don't want to hassle him because it does not affect his work or our family life adversely," Jasmine said.

"Sid fits the pseudo-developed category all the way," remarked Savannah when these types were explained to members of the club. "On the outside, he really has it together, but every once in a while, I glimpsed the insecurities that he hid from the rest of the world. He drank heavily—not in a casual, social way, but with a desperate fervor, downing one right after the other. One day it came to me: He was literally trying to drown his sorrows."

Many of the pseudo-developed men in the Farrell and Rosenberg study denied any problems. However, they reported symptoms such as having foggy minds, eating less, finding it harder to accomplish tasks, feeling less hopeful about their future, feeling despondent about their children maturing, and having difficulty making decisions and sleeping—all indicators of depression. Denial also played a part in their self-medication because they were the least likely to report excess drinking episodes. Nevertheless, they did admit to having less satisfying sex.

Several Midlife Wives Club members suggest that wives and children seek help for themselves through Al-Anon and Al-Ateen. (See the Appendix to locate local groups.) Katie and others believe that the concepts they learned in these support groups that helped them deal with a substance abuser also served them well in coping with a midlife crisis spouse.

Bear Crossing: Midlife Depression and Abuse

Like alcohol abuse, abusive behavior is a sign of psychosocial distress in men. Domestic violence is about the control of one human being by another and may be more prevalent with the punitive-disenchanted men who comprised the most symptomatic of Farrell and Rosenberg's four groups. They had the highest scores on the Midlife Crisis scale the researchers developed, as well as on other measures of alienation. More than half were discontent with their lot, and a whopping 80 percent expressed the desire to "start over." They had the highest scores in depression and had difficulties with both their wives and children. They were not only unhappy, but they tended to blame their wives, bosses, other races, or religious groups for their problems. Many of this type married early, had job problems, and had been despondent for much of their lives due to childhood deprivation, neglect, loss of parents, and abuse. Since they felt trapped in their dead-end lives, they tried to control any part they could. While most people think of domestic violence as being physical abuse, emotional and verbal abuse may be more prevalent—and less talked about. This bid for domination often begins with words that undermine the other person's sense of self and create doubt.

"Jack would call me a bitch or crazy or stupid. Is that verbal abuse?" Heidi asked.

"All name calling is considered abusive because it objectifies the woman as a thing rather than a person," Elinor responded. "Batterers define their mates as objects. Stefan would claim he never loved me and that I was the cause of everything that had gone wrong in his life. He threw things at me, screamed for me to get out of his house, anything to keep me on edge and wondering what he would do next." Finally Elinor had to get a restraining order from the court. "With Stefan out of the house, I am getting stronger every day."

Emily counseled several members who were under a verbal barrage from men who believed the best defense was a strong offense. "If his insecurities lead him to make upsetting comments, you can respond, 'Sorry, can't listen to this,' and leave the room." Emily said she took Gabe's belittling for too long, but finally her spine stiffened and she was able to hang up the phone or walk away. "Eventually he learned that the old patterns wouldn't work anymore."

"Everyone thought we had the ideal marriage and envied our lifestyle," Betty said. "My husband was so inflexible, I said that he wrote a book on how to do everything called *The Book of Jonathan*. If I came up with a different plan, he would toss it out. Although he never admitted he was stressed, it was revealed by his vile temper. Outwardly he was so sure of himself and cocky, but it was a cover for a sad, hollow man underneath."

Betty suspected Jonathan had a pseudo-developed personality because like many verbal abusers, while he was charming to others, he secreted his abuse behind closed doors and used it to dictate her life.

Typical verbal attacks reported by club members include:

- "You're too sensitive."

- "You don't know what you're talking about."

- "You don't have a sense of humor."

- "Can't you take a joke?"

- "You're crazy."

- "You made me do it."

- "You're trying to control me."

- "You're trying to start a fight."

- "You're not helping me by getting upset."

- "Why are you taking things so seriously?"

- "What's the big deal?"

- "You think too much."

- "You're so paranoid."

- "Why are you so upset?"

The blame game is a typical scenario in many crisis households. Caroline said, "Sean also held me responsible for all his woes even though some of his accusations were so ridiculous it was almost funny." Caroline's problems escalated after Sean's income shot to six figures. "That's when he became a jackass from hell. I knew he was stressed to the max and I was willing to put up with more time away from the family, the weekend golf dates to make important contacts, even his shorter temper at home, but not messing with other women."

Under the guise of being the successful corporate executive, Sean hid his pseudo-developed personality behind a picture-perfect façade at work as well as at home. He expected a hot dinner no matter the hour, obedient children anxious to run into his arms, and a tidy home. To keep everything together, he had to be controlling and was often insensitive to the feelings of his family.

In *If Men Could Talk*, Alon Gratch suggests that while women often feel shame about their appearance and interpersonal relationships, men are more sensitive about their accomplishments—both in the workplace and bedroom. One way a man discharges his inadequate feelings is to criticize someone else or blame them for his mistakes. So when the husband comes home after a day when he performed poorly at work, he may be quick to find something to carp on—from his wife's hairstyle to the leftovers for dinner to the children's noisy playing. He is projecting his shameful feelings on her, but since she already has fears about her appearance or not being a good enough housekeeper or mother, she internalizes his criticism. But the bad feelings are not dissolved. They fester in both and later ooze out in other negative ways. She may give him the silent treatment, refuse his amorous advances, or lose her temper over something unrelated. As club members know, these fights can escalate in a matter of minutes—or months—with nasty attacks and recriminations.

Polly felt abused when Fred blamed her for his emotional upsets. "He accused me of having affairs (emotional or physical) when he was the one who had a major crush on another woman. How's that for projecting what he was doing on me? But I don't think I am the innocent victim. It was an unhealthy dynamic between the two of us. I didn't have good boundaries and accepted a lot of his condemnation because of my own lack of self-esteem." Polly said she obtained insight into their arguments by reading Suzette Haden Elgin's *You Can't Say That to Me: Stopping the Pain of Verbal Abuse—An 8 Step Program* and Patricia Evans' *Verbal Abuse Survivors Speak Out: On Relationship and Recovery*.

Just as the mates of midlife men try to figure out what they can do to solve the problem, they also wonder if there is something they could do to stop the cruel words. They may try being extra nice, appeasing the man, giving him more space, begging for forgiveness, but nothing works. Why? The abuser has already won his battle for control because she is groveling to get him to stop.

Josie said that once she no longer reacted to the verbal punches, the tide changed. "I'd shrug and say, 'Okay, whatever you say,' and let it go. Zach didn't like having the wind sucked out of his sails, but it rolled off me and I felt better."

While physical abuse is easy to identify and verbal abuse follows patterns of blaming and put-downs, emotional abuse is more subtle and reoccurs in cycles. Verbal abuse is usually part of the scenario. In the first phase, tension increases, communication breaks down, and the victim feels the need to placate the abuser. Next comes the incident that precipitates anger, blaming, and arguments. This may escalate to intimidation and more serious threats. This is followed by a period of reconciliation in which the abuser may apologize at first, then excuse his behavior and blame the victim for starting it. He denies the abuse occurred, or claims that the victim is exaggerating how bad it was. Finally there is a quiescent period during which the incident is supposedly forgotten and no abuse is taking place.

"When I thought about some of our discussions, I realized that we didn't sound like friends," Polly reported. "I couldn't imagine saying the words he used toward me to him or even hearing him say them to anyone else. Fred never tried to understand my point of view. He used every trick in the book to put me down, change my mind, even correct my grammar in the middle of a sentence. Sometimes he'd snub me, other times he shouted me down. But most of the time he'd get furious and stomp out of the room if he didn't get his way." Polly learned that these were controlling behaviors. "The really sick part is I started to believe I was as worthless as he claimed. When I was down and out, that's when he'd be nice and tell me he loved me. What Fred was really saying was that he loved dominating me."

Jasmine could never figure out why Rudy was always hurting her feelings. She tried to excuse his actions by blaming it on too many cocktails, or the fact that his mother died when he was young and he didn't know how to treat a woman, or that he hated his job. Most of all she reproached herself. "My father used to call my mother a 'stupid idiot,' so when Rudy put me down, I accepted it the way my mother did." Finally a counselor helped her realize that she had been harmed emotionally by witnessing her father verbally abusing her mother. "I didn't want my son to think this was acceptable behavior for a man or for my daughter to feel it was okay to treat a woman this way. Also, it truly frightened them. They didn't realize that Rudy hadn't meant it when he said something like, 'I'll kill you if you do that.' "

Andrea thought Clint fit the punitive-disenchanted profile and that he subjected her to unnecessary emotional abuse. Within a few days of announcing he didn't want to be with her any longer, Clint moved into the other woman's house. "He claimed he had no feelings for me and was in love with someone else. We live in a town of less than one hundred inhabitants so everyone knew our business. It got messy because Clint told everyone our problems had been going on for two years and many other lies." Even though Andrea knew everyone was talking behind her back, she held her head high. Clint's reaction was to be the aggressor. He tried to convince Andrea this was what she had wanted all along, that she had been impossible to live with, too demanding, and mean. He accused her of having affairs, which he had investigated. "I'd like to see the supposed evidence, because I never did. Then he'd pull hurtful stunts like asking me to check if I was still the beneficiary on his life insurance. I was, but then I had to worry whether he was going to change it in favor of the other woman."

Colleen characterized Rory as an anti-hero. "I read that anti-heroes dream about starting over, which he was able to do in Japan," Colleen wrote. "For a long time I didn't understand that blaming *me* for *his* indiscretions was emotionally abusive."

His Turn: Darryl

"How about an extremely honest admission? After reading about this online, I must admit that I'm the punitive-disenchanted type—something that I would have never acknowledged before my intense crisis. It stems from painful child and teen issues that created a vicious pattern I've followed throughout life.

"I am addressing my needs and desires for the first time ever—something my wife agrees is necessary if this destructive family cycle is to be broken. Our new awareness has brought some real communication for the first time—something she values above all else. She said, 'I've waited decades for this.' "

Some women may be able to find ways to excuse and deny verbal and emotional abuse, but a physical attack is more obvious and frightening. Physical domestic violence may be a problem in up to 16 percent of marriages. However, this does *not* usually first present itself in middle age, because the majority of assailants are men 18 to 35 years of age. Most of these men use alcohol or drugs on the day of the assault, so if a man begins abusing a substance or use increases, the family is at higher risk. Job issues at midlife may exacerbate the situation because unemployment is correlated with incidences of domestic violence. One study found that approximately one-third of assailants were unemployed.

Betty said, "I might have gone on accepting the verbal abuse for years if Jonathan hadn't lost it one night and grabbed my arm when I was chopping onions. When I released the knife, he picked it up and poked it under my chin. He dropped it, but I'll never forget the nasty look in his eyes. I never felt safe with him again."

Like Betty, many members reported that physical abuse was preceded by verbal abuse, and the reason they put up with the battering was that they had already been worn down and conditioned by prior emotional and verbal assaults.

Jillian, who now thinks Paul's behavior is representative of the punitive-disenchanted type, linked her husband's physical abuse to his drinking episodes. "When Paul began renovating our house, he said he didn't have time to go to AA. I didn't push him because he was so busy. Then everything came crashing down. If I asked him a question about buying something, he'd fly off the handle. I had to tiptoe around in the evening after he'd had a few beers. He's hit me, but only in a drunken rage, and then he freaked out because he'd done that. He's more afraid of his own anger than I am, but he hasn't dealt with it, and now I worry that it will happen again if he doesn't get control of himself."

Lee said that her marriage was never abusive until midlife threw James for a loop. "The first time it happened, I was in shock. We were having an argument—although I can't recall what it was about—when he hauled off and slapped me across the mouth, busting open my lip. Then he grabbed me by both arms and threw me out of his way, leaving bruises on my arms." James had only a limited set of defense mechanisms, one of which was to deny any faults in himself. So, when Lee's criticism struck a sensitive nerve, he reacted with a knee-jerk response. Even though the physical blows were upsetting, Lee reported that the emotional battering lasted far longer than the bruises.

"The next time he hit me was the last," Lee explained. "We had already separated, but he came over and I confronted him with what I learned about the other woman. When he denied everything, I started to walk away. James spun me around and punched me square in the right eye with his fist. I fell against the wall so hard that a picture crashed to the floor. Later he had the gall to say he didn't remember doing it, that I was making it up, but I was the one with the eye swollen shut as proof."

Lee said that mental abuse is worse than physical abuse. "Bruises fade, scars heal, but the mind and the heart are more fragile. Constant lying messed with my head. James would reassure me one minute, and then do something wrong the next. Lies are a form of manipulation. James told me what he thought I wanted to hear, convinced that he was protecting me. The truth was that he was covering up for himself."

In the end each woman has to assess why she is staying in any abusive relationship and decide when she would be better—and safer—on her own. Some are led to believe that they must like or need such treatment, or else they would leave. Others may be told that they are one of the many women who love too much or suffer from low self-esteem. Yet nobody enjoys being beaten physically or harmed emotionally, no matter how low their self-image. Club members report that the choice of leaving or staying can be complex. Often the abuser has all of the economic and social status. Leaving could mean living in fear and losing child custody, losing financial support, and experiencing harassment at work. Family and friends may not support the woman and don't believe it is as bad as she claims. Also, there is usually a combination of good times, love, and hope along with the manipulation, intimidation, and apprehension. Sometimes intervention by authorities and counselors will change behavior, but remember when one person scares, hurts, or continually puts down the other person, it is abuse. And nobody should feel they must continue to live under abusive conditions.

Club members offer a list of behaviors that are abusive and should not be tolerated:

- Does he pressure you for the exclusive use of your time and attention? (He may have wooed you by claiming he never felt so loved by anyone before, making you feel he needs you.)

- Does he expect perfection or ask you to meet his every need?

- Does he say critical or cruel things, use degrading words, curse you?

- Does he call you names?

- Does he deprive you of sleep while he abuses you verbally?

- Does he impose his feelings on you by saying, "You make me angry" instead of "I feel angry"?

- Does he always blame you or someone else? Is anything ever *his* fault?

- Does he claim his feelings are hurt when he is upset?

- Does he rant about injustices in many aspects of life from his job to the state of the nation? Does he claim everything is unfair?

- Does he check up on you frequently to see what you are doing?

- Does he check the mileage on your car?

- Does he demonstrate extreme jealousy?

- Does he question you relentlessly about where you have been and whom you were with?

- Does he keep you isolated from your family and friends?

- Does he prevent you from having a job?

- Does he accuse your friends and family of stirring up trouble?

- Does he control the finances and make you beg for money?

- Does he make you ask for permission to go anywhere without him?

- Does he hit, push, slap, or shake you?

- Does he ask you to engage in sexual activities you do not want or take you by force, even if he pretends he is playing around?

- Does he find the idea or fantasy of rape exciting?

- Does he threaten to kill you if you leave, then possibly dismiss the comment by saying it was just a figure of speech or he didn't mean it?

- Does he expect the children to do tasks way beyond their ability and punish severely (such as spanking a toddler for wetting the bed)?

- Does he threaten to hurt or actually hurt the children? (More than half of spouse abusers are also child abusers.)

- Does he threaten to harm or actually harm the pets?

- Does he excuse past abuse of someone else because the other person "made him do it"?

Even if only a few of these items apply, it may indicate an abusive relationship. Domestic violence is taken seriously in most communities today. If a woman feels she needs protection, she probably does. Domestic violence safety tips include:

- If a protection order includes provisions about the children, give a copy to the children's school or child care facility.

- Make extra copies and keep them in safe places.

- Show the orders to police officers to improve their response.

- Show neighbors a picture of the batterer and his vehicle so they can screen visitors and call the police if necessary. Batterers often gain access to apartment buildings by pretending to be someone else or by following tenants indoors.

- Develop signals for neighbors and friends to call the police, such as banging on the floor or wall.

- Arrange to have a relative or friend call every day at an appointed time.

- Enroll in a self-defense course and practice these skills.

- Obtain a private or unlisted telephone number.

- Be selective about revealing a new address.

- Use the caller ID blocking code when making telephone calls.

- Use an answering machine or call-trace when receiving calls to collect evidence of harassment for protection order violations.

- Make the home as safe as possible by changing the locks, adding dead bolts, or leasing an apartment that is not on the first floor.

- Remove sharp objects and weapons from sight.

- Keep a telephone in a room that locks from the inside.

- Purchase a cellular phone and keep it in a pocket or in an accessible hiding place. (Free cell phones that can only be used for emergencies are available in some areas for domestic violence victims.)

- Pre-program 911 or the number of a safe friend or relative into the telephone.

Plan and practice an escape route out of the home and a safety plan for the children. Also, keep a bag packed and hidden in a safe place at home, locked in a car trunk with only one key, or with a trusted relative or friend. It should include money for phone calls, money for transportation, one month's expenses, clothing, diapers, court documents, passports, identification (social security numbers, driver's license, welfare identification, family photographs), birth certificates, school and medical records, necessary medicines, credit cards, checkbooks, work permits, green cards, lease/mortgage payments, insurance papers, bank books, telephone/address books, car/house keys, and ownership documents for car/house and copies of financial documents if possible. Contact the local family court for information on how to obtain an order of protection and do so promptly.

If anyone feels she is in immediate danger, call 911.

See the Appendix for more books and resources or contact crisis counselors at the National Domestic Violence Hotline. Staffed 24 hours a day by trained counselors, the hotline provides crisis assistance, shelter information, and legal advocacy.

- Call: (800) 799-SAFE (7233)

- Toll-free number for hearing impaired: (800) 787-3224

Remember help is *essential* when someone feels she cannot cope with any level of verbal, emotional, or physical abuse.

CHAPTER 6

Dangerous Curves Ahead: The Dreaded Other Woman

Every man over forty is a scoundrel.

—George Bernard Shaw, written in 1907, age 51

"If I am not wrong, I'm being wronged," said Hera, the goddess, as she worried about Zeus' affair with Semele. Since ancient times the specter of the other woman has loomed over many marriages. The defining moment in midlife crisis—and the one that changes the rules for most members of the Midlife Wives Club—is whether the man becomes involved with another woman. While some wives will tolerate a wide range of midlife eccentricities, few are able to withstand the presence of another sexual object in their husbands' lives. For many she is the deal-breaker who shatters the marriage. Even though much anger is directed at the adulterous spouse, wives also feel deceived by a "sister" who had no right to take something that did not belong to her. Understanding the nature of this bosomed beast not only helps a wife come to grips with the flesh-and-blood reality, but also how to counteract her presence.

Lee said, "The other woman in James' life offered him freedom from responsibilities and nothing but fun, fun, fun! First she was fresh and new. He didn't know her stories, and she hadn't heard his stale jokes. She showed a keen interest in everything he said, and she had plenty to talk about besides the children and household matters. She was exciting because she was forbidden fruit. She was nonjudgmental, didn't complain, and came with no baggage or annoying habits. Also, she had time to go to the gym and hairdresser so she always looked her best. How could a tired wife compete with that?"

Lettie had been on two sides of the love triangle. "I was the other woman for six years. The only excuse I have is I didn't find out he was married for over a year. Then I believed his tales about a miserable marriage and his plans to leave her. I am ashamed to admit that he not only lied and manipulated me, but he also physically abused me. If I complained, he'd go home to his wife for a while to punish me." Eventually Lettie married a man who vowed he would never treat her in the same manner. Then came his midlife crisis and he took up with a younger woman. "Some part of me thinks I deserved it."

"I am in love with a married man—maybe he is your husband," wrote Nicole. "So I guess that makes me the reviled other woman. At first we corresponded online as friends, but over time love has grown. Recently we met and it was the best day of my life! Down deep I hope he will leave his wife and come to me. The empty nights are so hard. We can never spend holidays together, and I have to wait to share something exciting with him. I keep looking for someone who can be mine, but nobody compares because he is the most romantic, passionate man I have ever known."

This post infuriated Jasmine. "Remember, you have fallen in love with a known cheater. It worked for him once, why not again when he gets tired of you? The other woman can never be secure because he broke a trust with someone else to be with her."

Elizabeth Taylor says she learned the same lesson. "You always get back what you put forth. And I should have known that I'd get back exactly what I had done myself," she said referring to the fact that the great love of her life, Richard Burton, left her for another woman just as she had taken him away from his first wife. "You get what you give."

Mira confessed that she was the one who was unfaithful in her marriage. "At first I felt free and in control of my life, but soon a nagging guilt crept in," she said. Then she gave advice to men tempted to have an affair. "If you and your spouse are fighting, it reassures you that you have made the right decision. If you are getting along well, you'll have the monkey on your back—that's why the cheater often instigates arguments. Eventually shame is going to get you. Nothing is going to feel right—ever." Mira said she might not have suffered if she had taken the advice of a friend who warned her, "Don't do it, it will ruin your life. I wouldn't trade ten of my worst days now for one of my best days then." Mira wished everyone—male or female—considering an affair would think twice before causing so many people so much pain. "These attractions are like an addiction. You're chasing a rainbow. Stop immediately and pray this other woman doesn't let the cat out of the bag. If you think you are in hell now, wait until your wife finds out!"

Nora didn't think that most men felt as guilty as Mira did. "While some men feel remorse because they have been unfaithful, others don't care, or they cover their cheating by blaming their wife for not meeting their expectations in some way."

His Turn: Karl

"Some spouses are unfaithful, others neglectful. Both can be destructive. Both can lead to divorce. Neither is an excuse. Both are simply reasons. Reasons and excuses are not the same. If you suspect your spouse has cheated, don't force him to confess or eat crow. If you've cheated, don't unburden yourself by admitting it either. Confessing is often more harmful than helpful. Put your energy toward meeting each other's needs. If the damage hasn't been too extensive, the marriage might be salvaged."

Anthropology 101

Coupling is one of the favorite of all human activities. Yet while monogamy is considered natural—at least for a while—many men (and some women) do not shy away from the chance to experience multiple partners. In our culture when either a married man or woman has sexual relations with someone other than their spouse, they are said to be committing "the sin of adultery" and all the religious commandments have never been able to stifle that transgression.

In the 1920s Gilbert Hamilton, a pioneer in sex research, reported that 28 of 100 men and 24 of 100 women had strayed. Alfred Kinsey's famous reports that appeared in the late 1940s and early 1950s stated that over a third of more than 6,000 men surveyed were unfaithful, but Kinsey surmised his figures were low and that probably half of all men were unfaithful at some point during their marriage. A half century later these figures have not changed significantly. A survey, conducted by the University of Chicago's National Opinion Research Center in 1998, found that 25 percent of American men and 17 percent of women had been unfaithful. That translates to about 19 million husbands and 12 million wives. The 1993 Janus Report of Sexual Behavior estimated that more than one-third of men and one-quarter of women admitted to having had at least one extramarital sexual experience. Some current polls suggest the figure is closer to 50 percent.

Anthropologist Helen Fisher says that out of 42 ethnographies about different people past and present, adultery occurred in every one, whether they were living in tenements, mansions, or thatched huts. No matter the traditions of marriage or customs of divorce, religion or any cultural mores about sex, each society exhibited adulterous behavior, even where adultery was punished with death. Adultery is the major reason for divorce and family violence in America as well as other nations. Our human tendency toward extramarital liaisons seems to be the triumph of nature over culture, part of our ancient reproductive dance.

So why, when scarlet A's, public flogging, stoning, stabbing, beating, maiming, and shooting have all been meted out for philandering, do we feel compelled to do it? Anthropologists suggest that males are innately attracted by sexual variety. If a man has two children by one woman, he has genetically reproduced himself; but if he engages in dalliances with yet another woman and sires more young, he doubles his contribution to the next generation. Who seeks more sexual variety, men or women? According to Fisher, men pursued affairs to spread their genes, while females evolved two alternative strategies to acquire material resources. Some elected to be faithful to a single man in order to reap the benefits from him, while others engaged in clandestine sex with many men to acquire resources from each. Man is the natural playboy, while woman is either the Madonna (the wife) or the whore (the infamous other woman).

Divided Highway: Why Some Men Cheat at Midlife

Even though there is no precise science that defines how the changes in the brain of the midlife man motivate him to be unfaithful, we know that many men yearn to adjust the status quo, to make up for time lost, or to fill some unfathomable emptiness. That does not mean he will act on his feelings, or even define them as a need for another woman. The fact is that only a small percentage of midlife men have the quintessential crisis and not all of these end a marriage. Statistically the riskiest period for divorce remains between ages 20 and 24 for both American men and women. But because the baby boomers have watched many of their peers splitting with far more ease than any previous generation, they assume that the pattern will continue into middle age, especially at crisis time. We suppose that partners become bored with one another as they age or that they would find it easier to abandon their mates after their children have left home. However, most divorces occur during the height of reproductive and parenting years, although the more children a couple bear, the less likely they are to separate. Worldwide divorce becomes less frequent in older-aged groups, and according to Fisher, 81 percent of all divorces among women and 74 percent among men take place before age 45.

Even the seven-year itch turns out to be a myth. Young and childless couples are more often likely to form pair bonds (monogamous relationships), desert each other, and bond again. Parents with one or two children usually remain together long enough to raise their young through infancy, then divorce and select new mates. Interestingly, couples with three or more children tend to bond for life and aging couples are most likely to stay together, although some of each sex are adulterous during the marriage. Anthropologists define this human habit as serial monogamy. Divorce is more common in societies in which women and men both own land, animals, and currency, and both have the right to distribute or exchange their personal riches beyond the immediate family circle. In communities where men and women are not dependent on each other to survive, miserable marriages can end—and often do.

A husband will desert a wife who brings home a paycheck before he will divorce one who weeds his vegetable garden. A woman with a salary is less tolerant of infidelity than one dependent on her spouse for food. Sociologist Martin Whyte discovered that the old-school belief that partners who came from different socioeconomic, ethnic, and religious backgrounds had a higher divorce rate is not true. Still, similar personality traits, shared habits, parallel interests, common values, joint leisure activities, and mutual friends were the best predictors of marital stability. And, as the Midlife Wives Club's list of crisis triggers demonstrates, marriages are more stable if they took place at a mature age. Other preventative factors include being deeply in love, growing up in a close and loving home, and having economic security.

Soft Shoulder: Why Men Stray

Journalist H. L. Mencken said, "To be in love is merely to be in a stage of perceptual anesthesia." Many members agree that their spouses underwent a form of brainwashing. Some condemn the other woman for seducing their man; others reproach their husbands for making bad choices. Most yearn to understand what went wrong. Could they have done something to prevent it or was his behavior out of their control? Most of these women dearly loved their husbands and were profoundly hurt by their actions. Acceptance of the affair may be an indication that the marriage was flimsy anyway. So what motivates a man to betray his marriage vows? In their book, *What Men Are Like: The Psychology of Men and the Women Who Live with Them*, John A. Sanford and George Lough list eight reasons men have affairs.

The first is *loneliness*. When husbands and wives are separated due to travel or other circumstances, he may look for temporary comfort in another woman's arms. He may not see this as a real affair. Pining has a physiological component connected to the brain's attachment system. People become listless when they grieve for a deceased or missing mate. Some find it difficult to work or eat or sleep. Psychiatrist John Bowlby wrote, "Loss of a loved person is one of the most intensely painful experiences any human being can suffer." When this feeling is combined with the opportunity to alleviate the ache, a man who wouldn't be interested if he were going home to his own bed may feel compelled to have a "harmless" fling.

Evie's husband met his other woman on one of his extended international business trips. "Every time Robert was with her, he was thousands of miles away from me. Maybe it first started because he was lonely, but after that, he looked forward to being with her and neither of them had any responsibilities so they were always in holiday mode. He said, 'She made me feel like I was 17 again.' She also made him feel needed because I was so independent with my job."

Since timing plays an important role in infatuation, a man who feels isolated—whether he is physically away from his family or trying to remedy unresolved isolation issues from adolescence—may be ripe for an erotic adventure. According to Dorothy Tennov in her book *Love and Limerance: The Experience of Being in Love*, people are most likely to shower attention on a love object when they are looking for adventure, craving to leave home, displaced in a foreign country, passing into a new stage of life, financially and psychologically ready to share themselves, or ready to start a family.

Another reason for an affair may be something Jung called the *projection of the anima*, which is the feminine, romantic side of the male personality. Since the passionate enthrallment we feel when we first are madly attracted to someone does not last forever, excitement can be rejuvenated by falling head over heels in love with a new woman.

His Turn: Stan

"Pheromones, man, pheromones. This woman in my crosshairs is shooting them in my direction. Some people are just more receptive to them than others. Not an excuse, but a scientific fact. She is a NAO/POW (not-an-option/potential-other-woman), and my only protection is throwing all my energies toward my wife. I'm planning a surprise weekend vacation with her because I know we need to get away—or at least I do."

When a man thinks that this new font of desire for the other woman will fulfill what was lacking in his marriage, he may spout the speech so familiar to many midlife wives: "I love you, but I am not in love with you." He may go through a series of such relationships pursuing the elusive perfect woman. The anti-hero and punitive-disenchanted men—the two dissatisfied types delineated by Farrell and Rosenberg—might have the most trouble finding long-term satisfaction.

Michelle tried hard to understand what Ted saw in his other woman. "Over time he told me he liked her cooking, she brought him lunches, that she was amusing, charming, a smart conversationalist. He claimed she was a good friend and an attentive listener. He said, 'She understands how I feel.' All of that may be true, but that is exactly what he used to say about why he fell in love with me!"

Other men are driven by the *need for experience*. Since many men facing midlife crisis married young, they may be compelled to stray before it is "too late." After a dalliance or two, the man may come to his senses and realize how good he had it at home. Many of these marriages are salvageable.

Heather said that she was Tim's first real girlfriend. "He never dated anyone besides me. I was 20 and he was 19 when we were married. Before that, Tim always did what others—especially his mother, who was a real tyrant—wanted, at the expense of his own needs. By the time he was in his mid-thirties, Tim started complaining that he hadn't lived yet. He talked of places he wanted to visit and hobbies he wished he had the money and time to pursue. I used to ache for him, wishing we could travel around the world or make some of his dreams come true." Tim stayed in the marriage for a long time because it was comfortable. "Whenever I made demands, he said I was being a controlling bitch like his mother. In the end he wanted to manage his own life—not the one his mother or I wanted him to live."

Others feel the need to establish an identity separate from their wives in what Sanford and Lough call *personal psychological differentiation*. Like Tim, many midlife men complain about being smothered by their wives and feel their personality is being stifled. Jung described the importance of movement to individuation—becoming his own person—throughout a man's lifespan. A man frustrated by problems at home or work starts asking for "more space," which may be his way of fleeing stagnation and despair. Sometimes he thinks an affair is a way to assert the fact that he is distinct from his wife.

His Turn: Jason

"For a long time I've been so buried by obligations and responsibilities that I didn't know what I felt about my wife. I've told her that I'll do my part and made an appointment with a counselor. Then, this weekend, I tried to talk to her about some of my sexual desires and why, with all the turmoil between us, I didn't want to make love to her. She accused me of desiring another woman who I chatted with at a party. I admit she was attractive, but I have never fantasized about being with anyone else until now. Suddenly there are either a lot more good-looking women around or I've just had some mental cataracts removed.

"The hard part is that she wants reassurance in the form of more hugs, kisses, and telling her that I love her. We're so far apart that I don't want to give her false hope, but if I don't relent, she'll think I'm seeing someone else, which I'm not—at least not yet. Besides, if she pushes me to say words I don't feel, I'll resent her even more than I do already."

Sometimes the man is *married to the wrong woman*. The reasons for the marriage may have been expediency, an unplanned pregnancy, or family pressures, but he either never loved his wife or it never progressed to a mature friendship. This man, who may have pretended that everything was fine on the surface, also may fall into the pseudo-developed category. In the privacy of his home he may criticize his wife for the many difficulties that stem from his feelings of inferiority. He may excuse his impotence by blaming his partner for not turning him on. If he can find sexual satisfaction with another woman, that proves there is nothing innately wrong with him. In fact, he may have been denying serious problems in his marriage for years and he might actually be happier with someone more suited to his temperament. Several Midlife Wives Club members thought their husbands were involved with a woman beneath them socially and educationally. Marlene felt that Archer believed he had married her because their parents belonged to the same golf club and they went to the same church. Now he had picked the other woman because he could feel superior to her—both in age and economically.

Sanford and Lough say the sixth reason for men having affairs is *the need to differentiate his Eros side*. In other words, a man who may have married for more pragmatic reasons realizes what he has missed by not following his heart. He may have given up a "true love" because she was of the wrong class or religion or it interfered with his educational pursuits. When he allows himself to think of what might have been, a man may fantasize about an adventure outside of marriage.

His Turn: Woody

"I'm 51 and can't help but compare my wife to some of the beautiful women I see, and of course she comes up short. I wish I still found my wife attractive, but she is overweight, not interested in sex, and reminds me much more of my mother than the sweetheart I married. I keep it to myself because I am not cruel, but I often imagine myself having a relationship with these lovely ladies.

"What I want more than anything else in the world is one of these women to pay attention to me to prove I am not over the proverbial hill. The longings are so intense sometimes I feel like I can't stand it another minute. I fear I will lose my ability to get another woman if I wait much longer. I am in a state of self-pity because I can't have sex with a younger woman. And the hardest part is that I don't want to be like this."

Marlene saw Archer's affair as a chance to reinvent himself. "The other woman only knew what Archer chose to tell her about his past and marriage. He embellished his image, lied about me and his past, made himself out to be a hero and his wife a dragon. She offered him a shoulder to cry on. He also acquired another honeymoon without having to commit for life."

Another explanation for an affair is the *expression of unused creative energy*. Many midlife men feel stuck in a rut. Their jobs are dull; their children are becoming adults who don't need—or reject—their input. Excess creative energy may be expressed as sexual energy. Bonnie's husband, Nigel, had several career frustrations and was approaching early retirement from the military with no future plans. "He covered up his fears by becoming cocky, arrogant, opinionated, and full of himself. When we tried to make love, he had problems but said it was because I had gained weight." Nigel proposed swinging, but this did not appeal to Bonnie. The next thing she knew he was placing ads on the Internet for women he could dominate.

The most content group of men—the transcendent-generative—are often the ones who are creating works of art or discovering ways to give back to their communities. Perhaps imaginative outlets also provide some "affair protection" and keep a marriage more stable.

Sanford and Lough's final explanation is that the affair is an *outlet for sexual fantasies*. Many men indulge in some level of sexual fantasy, hence the huge industry in pornography that is mostly geared toward male customers. Most fantasies are private and not even shared with their wife, especially if she is reserved about intimate matters. Some men pay to act out their erotic whims with a prostitute; others find passionate extramarital partners. Several male members of the club confess they were tormented by imaginings of potential other women. While many had similar thoughts for many years, they became more extreme at midlife, which activated intense feelings of both anticipation and guilt.

Emily said Gabe started talking about wanting to spice up their sex life. "I went along with most of what he asked, even though some of it embarrassed me. But then he suggested having a threesome or foursome. At first I didn't believe it because he was the puritan who would blush at rude jokes, but when I laughed, Gabe got angry. He was serious!" Gabe went on to have several affairs after he left Emily. "The funny thing is that when we do see each other, he still reddens easily, acts shy, and plays a passive role."

His Turn: Adam

"My emotions have flipped to the out-of-control mode. I'd give anything if I didn't have these feelings for this other woman, but I do. The only solution is staying away from her, but because of my work, I can't avoid her completely. She's a potential disaster to my emotional health, if not my whole life. An affair, let alone a divorce, would cause devastation and pain to everyone I love.

"Even though I have never uttered a single word about another woman, nor do I ever plan to, my wife may suspect why I have been acting differently. I won't hurt her by talking about my thoughts, but I can tell she is concerned. I have told her a bit of what I've learned about midlife crisis and that I am trying to make my future more meaningful. That gives us some basis for discussion, and it is not a lie. I know that the other woman is merely a symptom, one my wife does not need to know about because I hope it will never affect her."

Brain Chemistry 101

Is midlife crisis caused by changes in brain chemistry? Does falling in love with another woman follow any of the same neurological pathways as depression? If a man has been unfaithful all through his marriage, every indiscretion cannot be blamed on the hormonal shifts at midlife. However, if a man strays for the first time between 40 and 50, the chemical changes that accompany aging may trigger a wide variety of uncharacteristic behaviors.

His Turn: Stan

"I know I have a strong dose of midlife blues and I'm going through a rough time. I can't stop thinking about this other woman, although I want to expunge her from my mind. I wake early, go outside and look up at the starry sky, and start bawling. I am feeling more disconnected from life every day. If this keeps up, I will have to seek professional help."

Stan is feeling the "intolerable, neural itch," which is how poet W. H. Auden described a man's sexual cravings. Researchers believe that the passionate emotional disturbance that we call infatuation or attraction may begin with a small molecule called phenylethylamine or PEA. Known as the excitant amine, PEA is a substance in the brain that causes feelings of elation, exhilaration, and euphoria. PEA is a natural amphetamine that revs up the brain. So while one man may reach for a pill or martini to numb his feeling of inadequacy, another may find flirting the best way to pump up his dwindling self-esteem.

Every aging man will face a change in his sexual arousal pattern, and many panic, believing they may be experiencing symptoms of impotence. In 1980, before Viagra, Edmond C. Hallberg told *People* magazine that a man who has erection difficulties one night might take up skydiving the next day as a way of escaping his frustration. Other distractions include new challenges like climbing a mountain, getting in shape, or even tossing in the quest for the gold watch and becoming a ski or beach bum.

Unable to face the fact that their sexual drive is diminishing, a few men project their dissatisfaction elsewhere by blaming their middle-aged mates. As their anxieties mount, they begin to think that the antidote may be a more electrifying, usually more youthful, woman. Trying to explain the eternal lure of younger women to older men, Barbara Gordon wrote *Jennifer Fever*. Before there was a reliable pharmaceutical solution, a slender, smooth-skinned woman 10 or 20 years younger than the "motherly" wife at home was a surefire way to stimulate the libido. But since the other woman has not evaporated with the advent of the potent blue pill, these "Jennifers" must have other irresistible attributes.

Wendy said that Chuck loved being a "knight in shining armor" but she had a good job and was self-sufficient, so she wasn't dependent on him. "Chuck's other woman was the needy type. She looked up to him like a fan. Later Chuck admitted that she came along at a low point when depression was clouding his senses. The endorphin rush from being in love made him feel alive, and he craved that feeling of power."

One of the subjects in *Jennifer Fever* suggested that "the greatest aphrodisiac is not oysters . . . it is a worshiper." When a man's confidence in his virility is flagging and he may be feeling less powerful in the workplace, a woman who looks up to him because of his age and experience and also offers her embrace as proof of her devotion, is a heady cocktail that may prove irresistible because it fires up the brain's sagging PEA levels. Psychiatrist Hector Sabelli measured the amount of PEA released by skydivers before and after a jump. The PEA levels after landing were significantly higher. A divorcing couple also experienced a PEA arousal during tense court proceedings. PEA gives us a chemical high that accompanies a range of intense experiences from free fall to falling in love.

Oedipus Sex: Is It Still Mom's Fault?

Psychiatrists Harry and Melvin Prosen and psychologist Robert Martin of the University of Manitoba point out that Freud believed a boy's first love object is the sensual mother of his childhood. The midlife man may never have ceased his subconscious yearning for her attention. Although there is sometimes a resurgence of the Oedipal conflict at the time of puberty, some men also revisit the quest in middle age when they regress to earlier anxieties about physical adequacy, masculinity, and success. If a middle-aged man can win the attention of a narcissistically gratifying younger woman, he reaffirms his ability to attain an erotic object.

When the midlife man's wife reaches the age of the matronly mother he rebelled against as an adolescent, he may feel a compulsive need to revert to the maternal triangle by discarding the wife, who reminds him of the mother he left, and taking up with a woman who rekindles the primal spark he first felt in his young mother's embrace. Ironically, the idealized woman for whom he searches can never be found, but instead of being stymied, he may feel more compelled than ever to find her. The paunchy fellow with the Ponce de Leon complex, who did not sow his oats in the springtime of his adolescence, may act like Peter Pan, Don Quixote, or a midlife caricature on a quest for an elusive "Jennifer," whether she is Wendy, Dulcinea, a trashy babe, or a wide-eyed vixen.

His Turn: Harrison

"Why does a man of 45 seek a woman who is much younger? Perhaps because:

1. The midlife man craves excitement.

2. A younger woman makes him feel the age he was when he was sleeping with a woman that age.

3. A younger woman who looks up to him validates him when his own wife may have him way down on her list of priorities. Also the younger woman pays attention to his sexual and emotional needs.

4. He may be thinking with the 'wrong head.'

Is the eventual outcome doomed? Some men repeat their philandering, so you might as well let them go their merry way sooner rather than later and not suffer any more than you have to. For others the attraction usually fades as the crisis subsides, though it may take much longer to work through the pain caused to others."

Vim and Viagra

Erectile dysfunction, defined as the consistent inability to obtain or maintain an erection of sufficient quality for satisfactory sexual intercourse, is a symptom, not a disease, but it also can be the first sign of a medical problem. Although impotence is not a necessary consequence of aging, its incidence increases with age because the condition is often a side effect of other ailments that accompany getting older. In 1994, the *Massachusetts Male Aging Study* revealed that of 1,700 men ages 40 to 70 years, 52 percent reported some incidence of impotence. It is estimated that 30 million men in the United States suffer from erectile dysfunction, and that 95 percent of those cases can be treated. Although psychological issues—especially depression—are a factor, hormonal changes may have significant effects on erectile function, and there is a high correlation with illnesses that plague midlife men including heart disease, high blood pressure, and diabetes. Even though there are excellent medications to minimize these conditions, impotence is a common side effect of some of the medications designed to keep a man healthier.

The main causes of erectile dysfunction in the midlife male include:

- Depression, anxiety, problems with self-esteem, anger, fear, and other mental conditions.

- Diabetes, which affects blood flow through narrowing of the arteries or damage to nerve endings in the penis.

- Vascular diseases, such as hardening of the arteries or heart disease, which may lead to reduced blood flow, thereby impairing the ability of the penis to become sufficiently engorged to maintain an erection.

- Alcoholism and recreational drugs—including marijuana—which reduce the supply and circulation of blood to the penis.

- Prescriptions as well as over-the-counter drugs, especially those to regulate blood pressure, to lower cholesterol, to combat prostate cancer, or to fight depression.

- Chronic tobacco use which can narrow the arteries in the penis, reducing the blood flow necessary to maintain an erection. Even two cigarettes will markedly decrease the blood flow to the penis if smoked before sex.

- Insufficient testosterone or other hormonal imbalance.

- Pelvic surgery or radiation to the prostrate, bladder, rectum, or colon, which may cause nerve damage in the surrounding area. This may interfere with signals that must pass between the brain and the sexual organs that allow erection and orgasm.

- Injuries caused by accidents, particularly accidents associated with bicycle riding, water sports, gymnastics, and horseback riding.

- Injuries to the spinal cord or brain, or neurological diseases, such as multiple sclerosis or Parkinson's and Alzheimer's disease.

For thousands of years men have quested for the perfect aphrodisiac, but baby boomer men are the first Viagra generation. Viagra (Sildenafil) works directly on the blood vessels, allowing the arteries to expand, and only causes an erection when the man is sexually aroused. Other treatments include intra-urethral pellets, penile implants, penile injections, and vacuum therapy. Additional oral and cream medications are in the pharmaceutical pipelines, but it is Viagra—which is extremely effective with few side effects (except to the pocketbook because of the high cost)—that has resurrected the sex lives of more than 16 million men worldwide, including 10 million American men.

Midlife males are often snared in a catch-22. Aging predisposes them to medical conditions that can lead to sexual dysfunction. The medications for these problems also may contribute to their performance problems. A multitude of psychological, social, and hormonal factors may prompt depressive symptoms, and the medications that cure depression also may include impotency as a side effect. The reported incidence of erectile dysfunction may be over 40 percent for such popular drugs as Prozac and Zoloft. So when the confused, beleaguered midlife man feels beset with a resurgence of adolescent despair and struggles with worries about his potency and unresolved sexual conflicts, he may look outside his home for a cure. He begins to think another woman might extricate him from his morbid world of self-defeat, his downward spiral of feeling older, or his sexual vulnerability.

His Turn: Harrison

"What to do when your guy has an affair, by type:

1. **The Man's Man:** The guy who sleeps with as many women as he can and brags to his buddies about it over beer because the 'old lady' doesn't meet all his needs. Note that the wife is the last to know about this. When confronted, this type of man then blames her for his actions. When he gets caught, he hangs his head and comes home, promising never to do it again, but he's bound to repeat the cycle as many times as he

can get away with it. Divorce him! Otherwise he'll cheat on you for the rest of your life.

2. **The Missing or Lost Man:** The guy who feels trapped in an unrewarding situation but hasn't acted on it until now. He needs the other woman's arms for comfort. If she fulfills something that has been missing, he may never want to return home. When this man is caught, he'll come home and promise to never do it again. But then he will. The wife has to decide when she's had enough of his empty promises. If she lays down the law, he may stop, but it is not likely. He'll still be chasing skirts in the retirement home as long as he can wheel his chair around.

3. **The Seeker:** The guy with low self-esteem who needs to learn to like himself and being in another woman's arms helps for a while. When his wife files for divorce, he may come to his senses, realize what he's losing, and save his marriage. Both the Seeker and the Missing Man need space, so back off, work on your own issues, and prepare for a year of sheer hell. A patient wife can win either one back if he doesn't continue to mess up his life and if she wants him back.

4. **The Leaver:** This guy gets so fed up with his current situation that once he slams the door behind him, he does not waffle or look back. He may use midlife crisis as an excuse, but the bottom line is that he wants out of the marriage. Let him go. A few are able to handle the situation with compassion and caring (if that's possible), but quite often he follows the course of least pain for him, which is to walk away. Sometimes he remains involved in his kids' lives; other times he deals with the sorrow by pushing them away as well. Any way you cut it, this guy is not coming back.

5. **The Idle Cheater:** This guy is trying to satisfy specific needs in his life and sometimes gets caught up in a moment and wants to stay with his new partner. Sometimes he comes to his senses but not until he has had at least a taste of forbidden fruit. He needs help, but also a line drawn in the sand. The wife should offer forgiveness for one transgression, but if he does it again, dump him.

6. **The Family Man:** He feels it all, he suffers, but he sticks with his family and plays the cards he's dealt come hell, high water, or midlife crisis, with the help of a caring spouse. You don't hear too much about this guy, but I envy him. Be nice to this guy. He isn't going anywhere, although he might have fantasies. Give him lots of TLC and he'll be yours forever."

Gotcha! Uncovering His Affair

According to Sanford and Lough, keeping an affair a secret requires effort, adds stress—not to mention a frisson of excitement—creates endless complications, as well as forces the man to be in a perpetual state of deception. "Love affairs send out a kind of psychological fragrance—or odor as the case may be—and other people who are sensitive to such things 'sniff' out an erotic involvement between two people." Sanford and Lough continue, "Moreover, a woman who is tuned in to her husband, especially a woman who is close to the unconscious, can pick up her husband's errancy in love in spite of his best efforts to keep it secret. It is by no means unusual for such a woman to have dreams about her husband's love affair, and I have known cases in which the woman dreamt of the actual other woman who was involved. In addition, there is an attempt on the part of the unconscious to bring the matter into the open. Eventually some mistake is made that gives away the secret: The man leaves his mistress' phone number around, or a letter from her is found in the pocket of his coat when his wife takes it to the cleaner. In all sorts of sometimes ridiculous and unlikely ways the unconscious plays a trick and the affair is brought into the open."

Annie sensed Larry was cheating before there was any tangible evidence. "For a long time I convinced myself I had an overactive imagination. But there was something haunted in Larry's eyes when he looked at me, an off tone in his voice when he was hiding where he was going, even the way his hands felt." Annie remembered times he brought her special gifts or was especially helpful and she would recriminate herself for not trusting his love for her. "When you find out you've been deceived, you lose confidence in your ability to figure out who is scamming you and who is not."

Megan's husband, George, worked with his other woman for ten years. "She joked that part of her job description was to 'keep him happy.' People would ask me if I was uncomfortable with that," Megan said, "but I'd shrug it off thinking they were being dirty-minded. When I found out about the affair, I felt like a complete fool!"

Michelle's husband's assistant also became his other woman. "Ted was able to contain the story until she moved to another state. Suddenly there were late night phone calls, cute cards, and letters." Ted locked them in his briefcase, but forgot that Michelle knew the combination. "After I steeled myself to check on him, I was numb with the shock, but no longer naive. I spent a month gathering receipts, phone bills, and letters before I confronted him. Even so, he tried to deny it. I told him to leave and he did. Two weeks later he begged to come home." Michelle agreed so long as he promised to end all contact with the assistant, go to marriage counseling, and work toward better communication. "I did my part by forgiving him and he kept his word. Our marriage was salvaged—at least for a few years. Then he started all over again with someone else."

"I should have known!" Amanda wrote. "It was almost like Colin was leaving me breadcrumbs to find, but I guess I wasn't ready." To warn other Midlife Wives Club members she made a list of her husband's worrisome behaviors:

- Going out but refusing to say exactly where

- Coming in and *not* saying whom he was with

- Refusing to let her go with him

- Going for a drive to "clear his head"

- Receiving suspicious phone calls

- Taking his cell phone outside to make a call

- Being protective of the cell phone in case she should read a text message first

- Having a certain look on his face. It's hard to describe, but when you know the person you learn the expression.

- Lying about the reason for being with this woman. He'd say she was "just a friend" or he was out with some friends "for laughs."

There were other clues, too. Amanda found receipts in her husband's wallet for presents that were not for her. Suspicious, she checked the number of condoms in his drawer, wrote down the amount, and then counted the number he used with her. The figures did not add up.

Unfortunately Amanda's sleuthing paid off. When she went away for the weekend, Colin told her he was going to cook a meal for some friends from work. "I came home to find purple flowers on the table, purple candles in the living room, new CDs in the stereo, and even a new purple cover for his mobile phone. Purple is *her* favorite color, not mine! Also he had 'thoughtfully' changed the sheets. No wonder there were a lot fewer condoms in the drawer!" Still Amanda did not confront Colin. "I wanted more proof so the next day I went through the garbage cans. There I found a bag from a lingerie shop plus a torn-up letter from him to her explaining how he felt about her. Apparently he did not send it, but now I had hard evidence that our marriage was a sham."

"I probably felt more guilty for checking up on Larry than he did cheating on me," responded Annie when club members were discussing how they learned about their husbands' infidelities. "I knew he had been lying to me about his spending, but avoided dealing with the issue. After I found the receipts for jewelry and lingerie, it felt as if the earth had stopped turning. I was in a circle of darkness and thought I was going to fall into the void."

Even though Michelle suspected another woman, Ted denied it and said he was moving out to have "more space to think about his future." Michelle had some evidence, but he never would admit anything. "I could not stay in a marriage where I had lost all trust. It wasn't until I filed for divorce that he came out into the open with his other woman. Ted still won't acknowledge that he lied to me!"

Cyber-sighs

Once it took a lot of energy to meet a significant other; now it may take only a few clicks of a mouse. Only a few years ago online liaisons were unheard of, but today almost everyone knows someone who met a partner via the Internet. A midlife man who was never able to communicate his emotions verbally may find it easier to let feelings roll off his fingertips and connect with a cyber mate.

Naomi became concerned when her 36-year-old husband, Gilbert, began logging into Internet chat rooms. He started in the "married but looking" section, then graduated to instant messaging with some of his favorite online ladies. "Gilbert told me I'm a wonderful person but that he wants to find his soulmate—he used to say I was his soulmate!"

Willow said, "Glenn would rush to his computer early in the morning, then again as soon as he got home. One day I stumbled upon e-mails from another woman saying she longed to hold him in her arms. When I confronted Glenn, he claimed the message was meant for someone else. That's when I began snooping. The same woman *was* a regular correspondent, but there were many others, plus visits to chat rooms and pornographic sites. I blame the computer for making it easier for a man to cheat."

Evie's husband, Robert, started to flick the screen off every time she came near his computer. "I suspect he is chatting with someone he doesn't want me to know about. I know there has to be something going on inside his computer, but what? I need to find out!"

"I felt horrible for spying," Elinor admitted, "but I also was desperate to know so I purchased the sort of program that allows parents to monitor their children's online activities. There are plenty of spy programs available such as Starr, Spy Agent, iSpy Mail, or Spector that let you see what someone's doing online whether they're in a chat room, visiting a forum, or using instant messaging programs such as ICQ or IM. The programs log keystrokes, user names, passwords, path names, access times, window titles, as well as both sides of a chat conversation into a password-protected encrypted file. They can run in stealth mode so the tracking does not show up in the computer's system tray, task bar, or task list, and with most programs, you can set them to start automatically each time the computer is turned on. If you want to do remote surveillance, you'll want a program that can invisibly e-mail the log file to another PC via any standard e-mail account or that will save the log directly to the server. A couple words of caution if you're planning on using spy software: If you use a monitoring program secretly, make sure that you sign out when done looking. And while these programs are not easy for the average person to find, using one to spy on someone who is technologically savvy could backfire."

"I found out all I needed to know—and it was not good—by checking his e-mail folders," Vanda admitted. "Unless he empties the trash in the e-mail program (which is different from the trash on the Windows desktop), deleting the e-mail does not get rid of it. Oliver never took out the trash at home, so why would he bother on his computer?"

Jasmine had another method for checking up on Rudy. "We share a computer, so it was fairly easy. The default setting for sending an e-mail is to put a copy of what was sent into the 'Sent' folder. This is where you can read messages he originated. If you know his e-mail account name and password, you can check his incoming e-mail remotely. If it is web-based e-mail like Yahoo, Netscape, or iVillage, go to that website, select mail, log in, and have a look. If the e-mail is through a regular provider, like AT&T or Earthlink, use a service such as *www.thatweb.com* and fill in the blanks. In both cases, be careful not to delete what you are looking at." Jasmine explained that the problem is learning his password. "Many services have a method of retrieving e-mail passwords. They usually send it to another account or ask you to answer a question (mother's maiden name, favorite pet, and so on). If you know the information, you might be able to recover his password. Be careful, though, as some services will send the password to the account's registered e-mail address which may be a big tip-off if he sees the e-mail before you can delete it. If you don't know the password, you can purchase a recovery program like iOpus Recovery that ferrets out hidden passwords. This is less obtrusive than having monitoring software running on his computer."

Vanda added, "With Microsoft Outlook or Outlook Express, go into 'Properties' and set it so that it leaves a copy of the inbound mail on the server for a certain number of days. Normally, this is deleted from the server as soon as it is downloaded, but in the snoop mode, it can be set to remain on the server for several days. Then, using *www.thatweb.com* and knowing the user name and password, the mail can be read even though he has deleted it from his computer."

Lindsay said Malcolm started a cyber affair that escalated into a divorce, but she would have been in the dark for ages if she hadn't become suspicious. "I'm not sorry I snooped because it enabled me to protect myself financially when I read that he was going to move some bank accounts to position himself for leaving me. But Malcolm is a bit of a geek and knew how to cover his tracks." Lindsay explained how to go to the Microsoft Outlook "Inbox" organizer area and add a rule that puts a copy of every e-mail into another folder, or auto forwards it to another account that you control. "I opened a new account with Hotmail. Then, I auto forwarded duplicates of his mail to my account. I had to be careful, though, because if he ever went to delete his sent e-mail, he'd see some going to this new account. That meant I had to keep going back in to do housekeeping in his computer. At some point I didn't care if I was caught, because by then, I knew what he was sending and receiving from the other woman. But since he could see the extra folder as well, both of these tips can be risky if you're not ready to tip your hand or deal with a confrontation."

Vanda suggested looking at the browser history. "If you see websites that you don't recognize, click through them. You might find a chat room, or maybe a forum like this one. Some sites have voice chat that requires a sound card, but it is like using the phone and you can't read the conversation." She also mentioned checking his web browser's address bar or the history button. "If those are cleared out, then he is likely hiding something because most people don't routinely clean these."

Elinor added, "Learn more about 'cookies.' They are stored in a folder in the Windows subdirectory and are usually named after the website that was visited. You might be able to ascertain the last time he went to a website by the date on the cookie that is associated with that website."

"The main thing about snooping is that he can't know that you did it because it only takes minutes to set up a new account once he thinks you're on to him," Lindsay contributed to this controversial thread. "If you are logging in to view his e-mail, make sure that you sign out when done looking; otherwise when he checks his e-mail, he will get an error message or a notice that he is already logged in to his account."

Elinor said, "Finding out what I needed to know prevented me from being completely blindsided by Stefan's infidelity. It still came as a shock, but not as much as if I had heard about it from someone else or even from him when I had been unprepared. This way when the time came to talk about the abysmal state of our marriage, I knew where I stood."

Colleen said she stayed with Rory despite months of rejection, the discovery that there was another woman, and empty promises. "One night after Rory swore it was over, he was on a 'business trip.' Something was bothering me and I checked his computer, where I found an e-mail begging her to meet him that evening and to continue their relationship. He mentioned spending time with her when he had supposedly been away on family business one month earlier." Colleen waited up all night, and when Rory came home, she confronted him. "Rory swore he met with her to say good-bye and that they hadn't slept together. 'It's time to work on "us" now,' he said. At that point I lost it. I sobbed and pounded him with my fists, but I didn't beg or plead. Now we are talking about another reconciliation, but I doubt it will work."

Bothered, Bewildered, and Betrayed

When a poll on the topic "What's the one worst part about an affair?" was posted on the Midlife Wives Club website, 82 percent of those responding said it was the pain of the betrayal. And the betrayal wasn't always just by the polltaker's spouse. Sometimes the other woman turned out to be a person the wife knew and trusted.

Sheryl was married to Luke for more than 25 years and they shared a plumbing supply business. For more than a year Sheryl had groomed a woman to take over most of her duties so she could supervise building their dream house on a lake. "A few weeks after we settled in, Luke claimed he hadn't been happy for 12 years (where was I all that time?) and needed to 'find himself.' He leased a one-bedroom apartment and told me to keep all the furniture because he would 'sleep on the floor.' Then our daughter returned from a visit and reported that there not only was a new king-size bed, but the office manager had moved in!" The other woman's husband was Luke's best friend and both had been like an aunt and uncle to their daughter. "I was so shocked by the disloyalty that I felt like every blood vessel was going to burst."

Katie, who had been through something similar, counseled Sheryl. "You are suffering from having your self-respect undermined. That's what happens when you are betrayed. It may seem impossible, but you must find a way to speak to them both—either together or separately—and let them know exactly how you feel and where you stand. They need to be accountable to you and your daughter. It may seem like an impossible task, but you will feel better about yourself once you have stated your feelings."

Ingrid was stunned by the sudden admission that there was another woman in her husband's life. "I'm sick of being the one who has to hold everything together, deal with the kids, sort out the house. I'm tired of trying not to put him down in front of the kids, being civil with him when they are around, being reasonable in general. I want to be over this anger. I want to be indifferent to him and not feel like I want to shoot the other woman. I want to not mind what he thinks of me. I want to be able to see some value to the years we spent together. I don't want my memories to be obliterated by bitterness. Will I ever be able to trust anyone again? He wants her to meet his children but even the thought makes me ill. Reading the threads at the club, I know that life does improve eventually. Anyone have a fast-forward button to transport me to a time when I will be happy and over him?"

No matter how a wife finds out about the other woman and the affair, the pain is excruciating. She has been rejected and betrayed. She must face her worst fears and insecurities. Sometimes her first reaction is anger and she wants to do something to lash out at the man—and woman—who have conspired to hurt her. Other wives become frightened and depressed. Children are unwittingly dragged into the fray.

CHAPTER 7

The Littlest Passengers: Helping Children Cope

The value of marriage is not that adults produce children,
but that children produce adults.

—Peter De Vries, written in 1954, age 44

"Last week Davis told me he did not love me and wanted to live without me. Period. End of story," Crystal wrote. "Our children took it hard. When my youngest daughter confronted her father, he claimed he never said those words and he was trying to keep the family together. Since we hadn't separated, Davis said I should never have told them because they believed we had a perfect marriage and wanted to be 'just like us.' Now I am confused. If he is leaving, don't they have a right to know?"

If wives are confused by their husband's midlife changes, children are even more puzzled. Worse, they often feel that their dad's dark moods, angry outbursts, or absences may be connected to something they said, did, or didn't do. And just as midlife fathers often blame their wives or at least criticize them unfairly, children are disciplined when they happen to be in the way. Children bring noise, confusion, and messes; they take time away from personal pursuits; they are an expensive long-term commitment. The overwhelmed man may see his progeny as additional albatrosses to his freedom. Yet while it may be difficult to leave a long-term marriage, it is almost impossible to sidestep the children entirely.

Caution: Children at Play

Midlife Wives Club members agonize about the toxic spillover to their blameless children. When should they be told? What do they know or suspect? How is it affecting them? Some parents believe that their children are ignorant until they are told or until Daddy moves out. Actually, young children sense tension and may intuit an impending crisis even before Mom comes out of her denial phase. Some children may wonder whether there is something they could do to repair matters. Many reproach themselves thinking, if only I had behaved better, Dad wouldn't be acting this way or Mom wouldn't be miserable. They may also blame their mother, believing there has to be something she could do to make everything go back the way it was. Or they are furious with their father for destroying their happy family. Older children will worry how to tell friends or how relatives will accept it. Many question, 'how could you both do this to me?'

One misconception about child development is that children do not experience emotions the same way adults do, but they are able to comprehend logical thinking. In fact, the opposite is true. Even babies have the basic emotions of love, anger, fear, loneliness, and happiness. Others, like shame and guilt, develop in the first few years as children learn what their parents expect. Small children can sense how their adult caregivers are feeling and behaving from the tone of voice used. Although the jury is still out on the nature-versus-nurture debate—and some aspects of temperament are considered genetic—much of a child's person-ality is formed by how they are treated in the first few years of life. Caregivers help determine whether a child grows up to be an optimist or pessimist, loving or cold, trusting or wary. If a parent of a young child is cranky and scolding, she may never outgrow her feelings of shame and low self-esteem. That same child may later continue to vent her hostility on others, further making her an outcast. Fortunately, most midlife crisis men do not have chil-dren in the most vulnerable toddler stages—but some do.

Tasha and Leon were challenged by having children at three very different stages. "Parenting had been fairly easy for us, but then our 18-year-old daughter moved in with the boy she had been dating only a few months and didn't continue with her plans to go to college, our 16-year-old son started getting in trou-ble at school on a weekly basis, our teenage daughter became prissy and teary, and our 7-year-old took the opportunity to gain attention by testing limits," Tasha said. "Add our unex-pected bonus baby to that volatile mix and it was no wonder that Leon didn't find home the sanctuary it used to be."

It is in their school years that children learn about give and take, how adults behave under pressure, and the meaning of honesty and character. Much of their learning comes from mod-eling their parents' actions. Children turn to the parent of each sex to help establish different aspects of their identities. It is cute to see a young boy imitate his father's gait, speech, or manner-isms, and want to join his father at work or play. A young girl sets her standards for men based on her father's personality and attitudes. So what happens when children find out their father is having an affair or leaves the home without providing adequate financial support? What do they learn from a man who is willing to discard his wife for another woman or is confused and irri-tated much of the time? A daughter will observe how her mother relates to a man. If her mother is cowed, angry, or depressed, how does that affect her perspective on marriage and relationships? A boy's first love for a woman is for his mother, and as we have seen, this younger version of his mother starts out as his romantic ideal—one that gets confused if he has not evolved beyond this immature phase in his psychological development by the time his own wife reaches middle age. If his father hurts his mother, will he feel protective of her and angry toward his father or will he side with his father and become an adult misogynist?

As Annie said, "If children see a parent being strong, then they too will be calm. I take strength from my own parents' example. They have been married for over 50 years—since they were teenagers—and I know that some of those years had to be tough. But they stuck it out through whatever midlife crises there might have been."

When we try to explain what is happening to children, we assume that they understand our words, but they often misinterpret them. While they may have strong feelings, they cannot follow complex reasoning. If a small child is told, "Daddy's in Chicago and he'll be back next week," he may nod sagely, but be perplexed. What is a day, a week, a year? How long until a birthday, a holiday, or the end of a road trip? Where is Chicago—the next street, the next house, another planet? Why would their father move to a different house, say he'll be back "soon," see them every other weekend? Children prefer consistency and routines. When this changes, their antennae pick up the nuances and they show signs of distress. Young children may regress by wetting the bed or wanting a pacifier. Older ones "act out" their inner tensions by lashing back at siblings, misbehaving, doing poorly in school. Teens withdraw, turn to their friends, run away from home, or start tempting danger in the form of drugs, alcohol, premature sexual activity, and other risky behaviors.

When a crisis is occurring, children hear angry comments, snide snippets, even witness physical fighting. Frantic phone calls to family and friends are overheard. Doors are slammed; meals are left uneaten. Dad drinks too much and falls asleep on the sofa. Mom goes to bed early with a headache. Adults who voice their problems in whispers and keep the discussions behind the bedroom door still manage to send out worrisome signals because children are highly attuned to their parents' moods. Preverbal children understand more than they can express vocally and can follow adult conversation better than anyone believes. Even infants recognize emotion in voices and can have visceral reactions to hostilities in their home. Eventually, parents do have to explain what is going on—a conversation everyone dreads.

A month before James left, their son, age nine, told Lee, "Mom, I'm worried about Dad, is he sick or something? He doesn't act like himself." When he did walk out the door for the last time, Lee kept it a secret for a few days. "He was already used to his father traveling for business, but eventually I had to tell him that his father might not come home to live with us. For months our son cried himself to sleep, had nightmares, crawled into bed with me, and had some bed-wetting incidents. I overheard him tearfully begging his daddy to come back home. When James decided on a divorce, I asked him to tell our son, but he refused and the job was left for me."

Evie said she told her children that she still loved their father, but could not agree with what he was doing. "They were 14 and 11 and understood because I had used similar words with them when I disapproved of their behavior."

"I read that my daughters might blame themselves so I made sure they understood that nothing was their fault," Ingrid posted. "My eldest, age 12, rolled her eyes and said that it was our problem—not theirs—but the 10-year-old burst into tears. I took them both to a counselor for a while, which seemed to help. I think we've coped about as well as could be expected, but my youngest daughter asked if I thought divorce was genetic because my parents are also divorced. She's already worrying about how this will affect her future relationships, as am I."

As divorce rates rise exponentially—voiding half of all American marriages—so has the social acceptance. Most people believe that children are resilient and that two loving parents—whether living together or apart—can accommodate their needs in a variety of custody and blended family arrangements. However, recent longitudinal studies suggest that this perception may be another form of denial. Over 25 years ago, Judith Wallerstein and associates began interviewing a group of more than a hundred children whose parents were divorcing. Many of the young people were followed into adulthood and the parenting of their own offspring. The results, published in *The Unexpected Legacy of Divorce*, contradicted some fundamental assumptions. These children, who struggled with fears that their relationships would fail like those of their parents, had to fight the imperfect models their parents had set for them. The study demonstrated that the children of divorce had a different life view than their peers who were raised in homes with stable marriages.

"Despite trying to shield my children, they were damaged by our divorce," confessed Emily. "My eldest is delaying her engagement because she doesn't want Gabe at her wedding. My middle daughter moved to another city so she doesn't have to deal with him. Although our adult son lives with his dad, he becomes furious when Gabe treats strangers with more respect and kindness than he does his family. If they had their way, the family would have stayed together, even as dysfunctional as it was."

Margot said, "We have three children and they want to see their father, but I don't want him coming and going whenever he wants, because every time Cameron shows up, I get upset. Still, I don't want to be too harsh because there is a chance he may still come home."

Megan suggested that the parents establish ground rules.

"What we decided was that George would visit with them every other weekend, take them to school Tuesday mornings, have them for every other school vacation, and half of every major holiday. We wrote everything down. My attitude was, you play fair with me, and you can see your kids whenever you want. I was pleased that George went the extra mile and began driving the children to school one or two additional mornings, which they liked and it helped me. He also phones them every night to say goodnight, unless he is on a plane, and then he tells them in advance he won't be available. When they are with him, I call his cell phone to say goodnight to them. The result is two happy, well-adjusted kids."

His Turn: Harper

"Here's a reality check for men thinking they can 'have it all.' Your soon-to-be ex-wife will not want to share custody. Deep down she thinks the kids are hers and you 'help'—which is probably true. You will get to see them every other weekend, maybe less depending on how hostile she continues to be and how trusting the other woman is.

"Due to your actions, your wife will feel justified. You will have to continue to pay to support them even though you hardly see them, and will get no credit for the support you provide. When you do something nice for them, you will be labeled a 'Disneyland dad.' When you want to spend more time with them, you will be called 'disruptive.' If you ask for something, you are not 'putting the kids first.'

"You won't be able to win their hearts or minds and they may never forgive you for breaking up their happy home—which is what, in fact, you did."

When Children Need Professional Help

"Last week Perry told me that he wanted a divorce, which came as a total shock since we were planning to build a house," said Doreen in her first post online. "The next night he told the kids that he no longer loved me, but he did love them, and this morning he moved to his mother's house. On the advice of my best friend, I went to see a lawyer, who was convinced that there was more to the story and told me to keep my eyes open. Well, now they are wide open! There were a lot of cell phone calls to a 17-year-old girl who is a senior in high school. I confronted Perry, who claimed he had been helping her with some family problems. The next day her parents found out and she confessed they have been intimate. Now the girl is going around school saying her plan worked and he's left his family for her! Here's the really sick part: Perry has been using our teenage son to see her. He's been going to high school football games with our son and meeting her there. This girl is only three years older than our eldest son and our son is upset about the gossip. Our 8-year-old has started wetting his pants, something he hasn't done for at least five years. Is this a 'normal' midlife crisis?"

Katie responded, "Something is terribly wrong with your husband. If nothing else, she's underage and he could face legal repercussions. Secondly, her behavior sounds Lolita-ish. She took him on as a challenge and now that he's left you, she thinks she's won some game and he's her plaything. She doesn't love him and will move on as soon as she's bored. You must get your children into counseling ASAP. Your little guy is sending signals that he needs help, and your older one may be at even greater risk because it will be harder to express his muddled feelings. Between your counselor and attorney, you will have to sort out child visitation issues because it may not be a good idea to have a normal schedule if this teen girl is going to be involved."

"Our son witnessed the emotional abuse Dimitri inflicted," Bettina wrote. "When he asked me why I permitted his dad to talk to me in such an ugly way, I explained that his father didn't mean it. He was having problems and suffering inside. Maybe I shouldn't have excused Dimitri, but that was also the truth. What worries me is that subconsciously our son may think it is okay to treat a woman like that."

Although parents don't plan to inflict pain on their offspring, marital upheavals are always traumatic to some degree. Some men—like Dimitri—are so caught up in their own drama that they don't pay attention to the effect their actions are having on their children. Others—like Perry—may be involved in inappropriate liaisons that can inflict serious psychic wounds. The child's stage of development, temperament, as well as the way the parents manage the changes will affect how well they function, not only during this transformation in their lives, but also through time as other family alterations (reconciliation, separation, remarriage, and so on) take place.

Children may need special consideration—even professional help—if they exhibit these warning signs:

- Exhibiting a loss of interest in activities they once enjoyed like sports or hobbies

- Becoming more withdrawn (spending more time alone or in their room)

- Experiencing mood swings (crying easily one minute, laughing the next)

- Being constantly sad (crying easily and often)

- Experiencing a change of eating habits (eating much less or more than normal)

- Experiencing altered sleeping patterns (either sleeping more or less than previously)

Pediatrician Dr. Robin Madden, who also has a Ph.D. in clinical psychology, says that all of these symptoms are normal when a child is in the midst of a family disruption. However, if these indicators last longer than a month, children may need additional help by a professional therapist or social worker.

Over the River and Through the Woods: Holiday Issues

Each holiday season, traffic online increases exponentially. Families in turmoil have trouble with traditions that dredge up memories of more stable times or the way things are "supposed" to be. Media images of families reuniting around the Thanksgiving table, coming home for Christmas, finding Easter eggs, or waving flags at the Fourth of July parade bring tears of both fury and sorrow to Midlife Wives Club members.

The day before her first Thanksgiving alone Claudette wrote, "I thought I was going to make it through the weekend, because the last couple of weeks I feel I have been doing better. We were supposed to drive to my mother's house yesterday, but suddenly my daughter decided to spend Turkey Day with her dad—and the other woman! I am devastated. Why am I the one who has to make all the sacrifices? The thought of my daughter sitting at *her* table, enjoying the meal with *her* cozy little family is making me crazy!"

Tammy tried to be conciliatory. "You have every reason to feel betrayed, but the upside of this is that the other woman is trying to make your daughter feel like she can still be with her dad. Whatever happens, try not to express any hateful behavior in front of her and give your daughter permission to have a good time with Daddy. By comparison the other woman will seem shabby."

"I can't believe that I'm alone in a big empty house while Evan has the twins for Easter weekend at his parents' home," posted Sasha. "Not only that, I won't be around for their fifth birthday! How did I end up with the short end of the stick? Three months ago we were together, then I got the 'speech.' For the children's sake, we agreed to act amicably and to split holidays, with Evan getting the first turn because I would have them daily. It made sense so I went along with his program, even helping build the girls' excitement for their visit to their grandparents so they wouldn't shed any tears when they left. When they asked why Mommy wasn't going, I said I was 'sharing them' with Daddy and his family. I forced myself to wave and smile as they drove away, then I fell apart. Now I'm planning a self-pity party with a good cry, a bottle of wine, and a long bubble bath."

"Being sad and upset is only natural," Lee responded, "but you did what was best for your children. I remember the first time James drove away with the children and the despair I felt seeing a little hand in the back seat waving good-bye. But they'll be back."

Christmas is the Everest on the Midlife Wives Club members' calendars. How will they survive the holiday season with their fractured families? The Holmes and Rahe Social Readjustment Rating awards twelve additional life change units for the holiday season, which not only brings the darkest days cosmologically but psychologically. Advertisers push expensive gifts, children dream of fabulous presents—but also that their parents might magically reunite so their life will be like the heartwarming scenes they are watching on television. If their husbands are absent, club members may be wondering how they will pay their household bills, let alone create a cheerful atmosphere. Depressed single moms may not have the strength to decorate a tree, bake cookies, shop, or fit the preparations into an already hectic schedule.

"Christmas is our big one," said Evie in Australia, "and I don't see how I will ever get through it. We're supposed to go to Robert's house because he won't leave the other woman alone and he wouldn't dare bring her here. I don't know how I'll get through being with him and her at the same time, although I'll try for the sake of the kids. Right now I can't even drag myself out to do the shopping."

Lee was sympathetic. "Last year I didn't decorate the house except for a small store-bought tree. This year my son and I managed the outdoor lights together, something that James always did with him. My son knew more about what to do than I did, so this was a double statement. I was allowing him to be the leader and together we are a different sort of family. That got me thinking that I should start other new 'traditions.' James didn't like the theater, but now I am adding local productions of *The Nutcracker* and *Scrooge* to our schedule. We're going to a tree lighting in the park and then cruise around and decide what home displays we like the best. Also, many people have it far worse than we do so we're volunteering at the nursing home. None of this is going to erase the bittersweet memories of our past, but if this goes right, it will help lay the foundation for some wonderful memories in the future."

His Turn: Ellis

"This year my wife refused to talk to me about what she was giving the kids for Christmas. Since I see them regularly, I heard some of the items on their wish list and bought many of them. Now it turns out she did as well and the children have many duplicates. At first I was upset because this could have been avoided if she had been willing to work on a list with me, but I didn't want the children to hear any carping between us. So I told them it wouldn't hurt my feelings if they returned mine and picked out something they would enjoy, and I would take them to do that if they wanted. The greatest gift you can give the children is a happy holiday, free from the conflict that their adults have created."

Even Midlife Wives Club members without children often feel lonelier at Christmas. Tish wrote, "I don't have any children and I couldn't get in the spirit. I'm too down to decorate—besides, who would see it? Then I realized that I was the one who did it anyway, so I took the boxes down from the attic and put out my favorite ornaments. Our special tradition was finding the perfect gifts for all our family members, with brainstorming and list-making culminating in a big shopping day together with an elegant downtown lunch. I will miss that."

"We've had some frugal holidays around here since Colin left," Delia contributed, "but the children don't notice whether it is a roast beef or roasting chicken. You can make your favorite stuffing, string popcorn decorations for the tree, bake cookies. My kids like the projects we do around the holidays and appreciate the time I spend with them the most. I also have a limited budget this year, but the atmosphere will be full of music, mostly homemade decorations, cocoa and marshmallows, and a roaring fire in the hearth. Hugs are much more valuable than stuff!"

Here are some club members' holiday helpers:

- These are your holidays. Don't let anyone or anything take that away from you.

- Don't let the situation ruin another day of your life—let alone a special day.

- Start a new tradition like inviting someone you know who will be alone.

- Try a "living tree" as a life-affirming symbol.

- Accept invitations so you don't have to be reminded of what the holidays were like before he left.

- Force yourself to do some of what you did in the past for the children's sake, or even your own.

- Don't think you have to go "whole hog" and knock yourself out for weeks. Conserve your strength, but make some effort.

- Don't try to do the "heavy work" like outside lights or big displays that your husband may have tackled.

- Make a realistic budget and stick with it. Post-holiday bills will only add to your problems.

- Even if you aren't churchgoers, find a Christmas recital somewhere. Music can be uplifting and joyous.

- Take advantage of free or inexpensive civic events like tree lighting ceremonies, downtown holiday decorations, or school plays. Zoos, museums, and even some corporations have interesting exhibits and events.

- Make gifts for friends and family with your children. Magazines offer ideas for jams, cakes, cookies, and simple crafts. (The library has books and back issues or visit Internet craft sites for ideas.)

- Look through your jewelry box or attic and give your children family keepsakes instead of store-bought presents.

- Thrift shops, flea markets, and church bazaars are places to find inexpensive items, and nobody needs to know where you found the gift.

- Find your "holiday smile" and paste it on for the children's sake.

- Volunteer! There's nothing like helping others to make your holiday better.

- Serve meals at a food kitchen or homeless shelter Christmas day. (You can eat there as well and not even cook.) It's also a good experience for the children.

- Even with a limited income, buy something for a more unfortunate child. Call your local foster parent's association, look for an "angels" tree at the mall, or watch the paper for needy cases.

- Take your children to visit a nursing home. Older people love seeing young faces, and your children will find the extra attention rewarding.

- Check out holiday-themed books from the library. They also have video and audio tapes as well as festive programs.

Merge: When Children Interact with the Other Woman

One of the most delicate issues arises when the other woman becomes involved with the children, which inevitably happens if the midlife man has a significant love interest and is separated from his family.

"Roger complained that dealing with our teenagers was too stressful. Now he and the other woman are contemplating starting a new family," Grace said. "He thinks they are more in tune about parenting issues, so this time it will work better. He feels our sons have not turned out well—and in so many words he has let them know it. His home is extremely rigid and if the boys do the slightest thing wrong, he punishes them. I don't want to interfere with the rules in that house, but the other woman—who is 20 years younger than Roger—told me she wants a 'normal' life without the 'complications of teenagers.' He doesn't use up all his visitation days and often drops them off early. When he does have them, he confuses them by trying to be a buddy—like giving the 16-year-old beer—but then demanding total obedience."

Stacey panicked when Norm warned her that he would be introducing their children to his paramour. "I became physically ill over this meeting," she wrote, "because it is another signal that our marriage cannot be saved. Why would he involve her with his children if he did not plan on her being a part of his life for a long time?" The day after the children met the other woman, Stacey reported, "When they got home, my daughter told me the other woman was sleeping over at her dad's. Then she went to my jewelry box and found my favorite necklace and burst into tears. She said, 'That woman has an identical one! I asked her where she got it and she said Dad gave it to her.' Does he think a 12-year-old wouldn't notice something like that?"

Club members understand how difficult it is to bring up these delicate matters with children when there is animosity over the other woman, but they support each other with ways to keep the paths of communication open. Annie pointed out that courts are interested in children's emotional well-being. "Sometimes a parent is prohibited from having overnight company when children are present. In some jurisdictions this can be written into separation agreements and divorce decrees."

"When I was a teenager, my father started a long-term affair, but my mother maintained an idealistic image of him," wrote Lee. "Twenty years later—with the affair still going on—I learned the terrible truth. It was worse to be deceived by both my parents than to have learned the facts earlier."

Children must be told what is going on, but they don't need every detail, only as much as they can digest. What you tell a child of 4 is quite different from one of 14. But as they grow and ask more probing questions, you must be ready with the answers. Madden says, "Give the child the opportunity to ask questions and answer only what is asked. For example, if a 2-year-old asks where Daddy is, you can answer, 'Daddy's not coming home for a while.' If a 10-year-old asks, you might say, 'Mom and Dad aren't getting along right now, so we've decided to spend some time apart. But both of us love you.' It is important to let them know that what is going on between the parents does not affect their feelings for the child." Madden warns that it is not smart to try to protect the child by saying nothing, because children perceive when there is tension and sadness in a household. "If no explanation is given, children may assume they've done something to cause the problem."

His Turn: Harrison

"No matter what happens, treat your kids well. If your marriage is over, don't expose them to a string of new girlfriends until you're divorced, or at least until the relationship is serious. Don't drag them into the middle of a romance or try to manage your relationship with their mother through them. The best you can do is establish even closer bonds and build on those to forge life-long trust and friendship."

Powerful Parenting

"Our life has been turned upside down for the past 15 months, and both my son, now 11, and I never know whether Derrick is coming or going," wrote Millie. "The other day our pastor preached, 'If you're in the driver's seat, get out and take the passenger's seat. Let God take the wheel now.' On the way home I told him that I was going to follow this plan because if we are the passengers we can sit back, enjoy the ride, and take care of ourselves. In fact, that's all we *can* do, anyway. The last time Derrick dropped the kids off, I was more relaxed, and we were able to have a civil conversation for the first time in months, which helped all of us feel better."

Emily and Gabe's children were 14, 16, and 17 when the mood changed in their home, and Emily believes they sensed the animosity early on. "The day Gabe left we had a family meeting. I told them he was depressed and this was coloring how he felt about many aspects of his life, except that he still loved them. I said I was unsure of what was going to happen but we'd work through this together. Soon we noticed the calm in the house—and we liked it. Whenever one of us started to bicker, someone would pipe up, 'No animosity!' and then we would laugh. I encouraged communication by teaching them to express their feelings using 'I statements' like 'I feel sad when you say you'll call and then you don't.' Also I didn't bad-mouth Gabe. Even in the angry times when I criticized his behavior (for instance not showing up to see them), I still tried to put the best spin on it (like saying he must have gotten delayed at work)."

Although children present multiple dilemmas, they are also a source of comfort and delight. Most are buoyant. Listening to their laughter and watching their progress can be uplifting. Giving them slack will also ease tensions, so pick battles carefully. Children in fractured families require more reassurance than ever before. The easiest way to do this is to "catch them being good." We don't normally compliment each accomplishment, but praise has never spoiled anyone. (Doesn't everyone feel good when their cooking is complimented or they are told an outfit is flattering? Aren't they more likely to take the effort with the next dinner or wear the outfit again?) Positive reinforcement is the single most effective way to manage children's behavior. If good behavior is noticed, they will try to please by doing more of the same—and this goes for toddlers to teens. Children whose families have been turned topsy-turvy by their father's crisis need extra comfort, but every child benefits from knowing they are appreciated. Children rarely do everything we want, but if we praise the part we do like, there is a greater probability of compliance in other areas too.

Positive parenting comments include:

- "Good job putting those blocks in the basket. Can you find a few more?" (Instead of: "You won't get a snack until you put the blocks away.")

- "Thanks for putting your dishes in the dishwasher. I need all the help I can get." (Instead of: "Why don't you ever help me?")

- "That sweater is a great color for you. You picked the perfect outfit for school." (Instead of: "You can't go to school with your hair like that!")

Neither the toddler, school-age child, or teen can always satisfy the parent, but noticing what they did right—instead of being annoyed about what they did wrong—has a higher chance of getting progressively better behavior. The parent can help with the final blocks, ignore the chore left undone (leaving the part the child was supposed to do for later), and hope that the hairstyle will change (they always do). The result will be more cheerful parents, children, and a less chaotic home.

Even young children can participate in the serious work of running a household far more than most parents expect. It takes time and a consistent plan to teach small children, but once they "get with the program" and understand that this is not about forced labor but about being a part of the family, they usually join in without too much griping. The younger they start, the better, but even if children have never been expected to do much, the crisis can precipitate a family meeting where the deal is changed.

Jasmine didn't want to further aggravate her teenagers by forcing them to do their father's chores after he left home. When depression sapped her energy, she needed their help. Her therapist suggested a family discussion that put the burden on dividing and monitoring the workload on the youths. "All you had to do was look around the house and yard to realize we were falling apart, so the kids knew we had a mess on our hands. I asked them, 'What do you think you could handle?' Their list was longer than one I would have prepared. One liked outdoor work and offered to keep up the yard; the other said she didn't mind the dishes or pots and would cook one big meal a week. They argued about whether the garbage was an inside chore or an outside one, then decided to split it by the week—and included every trash basket in the house, even toilet scrubbing. I can't believe they offered to do so much."

Elinor said, "Stefan believed that even young children can do far more than most people allow them and started them out with responsibilities way before I would have. By the time they were 3 and 5, they were loading the dishwasher and washing some pots in the sink. At 5 they could use the microwave for some snacks, make a cereal breakfast, and clean their messes. They knew to put laundry in the basket and picked up their rooms. This was a godsend when Stefan took a hike because they pitched in without me having to be the disciplinarian."

His Turn: Jared

"The most important point for me to remember is that my only true shot at immortality is through the memories of my children. I must make sure they're good ones. In order to do so, I am:

1. Cutting back on the rat race in favor of quality time with my wife (both in and out of bed).

2. Trying not to work too long or hard because life is short.

3. Stopping to smell the coffee *and* the roses.

4. Tiptoeing through this midlife minefield hoping I don't hear the click of a trigger mechanism."

Most children have friends whose parents are divorced. They know what "Dad's weekend" means and wonder if they will ever have to distribute their possessions—and loyalty—between two households. As soon as the midlife crisis becomes obvious, children will begin to worry about the stability of their home and need much more reassurance than many parents who are caught up in their own distress may realize. Once the resolution to the crisis is accepted, many mothers still can't forgive their husbands for hurting the children. Not every midlife crisis ends in divorce, but every child will have some negative legacy if there has been any upheaval in their lives. Sometimes this will be obvious while it is happening; other times the stress will reveal itself more subtly or at a later stage of development. Both parents must be alert and aware that their actions will influence their children, even if that was not their intention.

Besides dealing with children's and extended family issues, Midlife Wives Club members have to deal with numerous new and baffling scenarios when coping with a husband's midlife crisis. The next chapter offers advice on managing the first anguished minutes, hours, and months.

CHAPTER 8

Taking the High Road: Surviving Every Scenario

The beginnings and endings of all human undertakings are untidy.

—John Galsworthy, written in 1933, age 66

For her thirty-seventh birthday, James brought Lee flowers in a smiley face vase with a generic birthday card devoid of any mention of "love" or "wife." He had a dour expression and seemed distracted so Lee asked what was on his mind. "James stared at his shoes and mumbled, 'I feel dead inside. I don't know what I want, but it has to be something different.' " Trembling, Lee asked him if he still wanted her and he didn't answer. "He said he loved me, but he didn't know how much. He stated that he didn't want a divorce—yet. He grumbled that he didn't have anything to show for his life, that he didn't want to end up like his father, then he blurted, 'I will always care for you.' "

Lee sat down in shock, unable to speak or ask more questions. She was unprepared for the depth of his confession. James kneeled and placed his head in her lap. Lee hugged her husband and they both cried. "I told him that I understood—even though

I did not—and that we would figure this out the way we had worked through other problems over the years. He looked up at me and his eyes looked dead. That's when I knew our life together would never be the same."

Lee had known for months that something was wrong, but she never expected James was ready to leave her. Like Lee, many Midlife Wives Club members awake one day to find the other shoe dropped. Now what?

No Steering, No Brakes: When Rage Takes Over

Anger is often the first—and sometimes the most lingering—response to any shocking situation that upsets a life pattern, whether it is the diagnosis of an illness, a sudden death, or a disruption in a marriage due to a husband's actions. Anger is a normal, usually healthy, human emotion. When it flies out of control, it can spark bewildering reactions. This is precisely the moment when many women desperate to quell their anxieties find the Midlife Wives Club and cling to it like a lifeline.

Dr. Charles Spielberger, a research professor at the University of South Florida and past president of the American Psychological Association, specializes in the study of anger. He says anger is "a psychobiological emotional state that varies from irritation to rage." Spielberger suggests anger is a useful clue that "something is going awry and that we should act either by leaving or asserting ourselves." Anger also stimulates the autonomic nervous system to secrete the fight-or-flight hormones. Paradoxically, a woman's reaction to disloyalty may not be all that dissimilar chemically from her mate's response to the stress that led him to his crisis, yet each gender may respond differently.

Men are prone to physical gesturing and yelling, while women tend to cry and withdraw. Several club members said they curled in the fetal position for hours or couldn't get out of bed for days. Although some believe that venting provides healthy release, researchers found that acting out in anger increased heart rate, deep breathing, body temperature, and general agitation level. In fact, in studies of facial expressions and muscle activity, people who were told to act angry—even if they did not have any furious feelings—experienced physiological symptoms of rage.

Spielberger says there are two forms of anger: anger in or anger out. Overt rage—like screaming, battering, or waving a weapon—is anger directed outward, but anger does not always lead to loss of control. Social psychologist Carol Tavris, author of *Anger: The Misunderstood Emotion,* says that we lump the word "rage" with anger, hostility, and aggression. Because anger is a heightened state of physiological arousal "you cannot be in it permanently or you will die," she says. "Hostility is a disposition toward anger, and aggression is behaving with intention to harm." Tavris adds that anger "may lead to aggression or it may lead to baking a cake." Although rage can escalate to many forms of violence, some people endure extensive periods of fury and never lose control. According to University of Southern California clinical neuroscientist Adrian Raine, this is because most of us have a functioning prefrontal cortex that regulates aggressive feelings much like an emergency brake slows or stops a car.

"Give me the sticks and stones!" Heidi wrote in frustration, as she vented her barely restrained anger to the club. "I had to call Jack because I couldn't get my car out of the driveway and needed him to come over. He asked me not to phone him unless it was important, but how does he expect me to get to work and the kids to school with foot-high snow? He knew I've been in bed for a week with the flu, but said he 'might get to it tomorrow.' Meanwhile I was sure he was cuddled up with the other woman. So, I got out of bed and did it myself, fever and all.

When I was done, I collapsed on the couch. This is the first time I've cried in a long time. Sometimes a hug or touch is all I want. Other times I need some real help around here. Either way, I am 52 years old and have nothing."

Interestingly, Heidi's surge of anger may have elevated her heart rate and blood pressure, and boosted the level of her energy hormones, adrenaline, and noradrenaline, which enabled her to tackle the physical task, whether prudent or not. These temporary bursts of vigor allow us to survive emergency conditions, but they come at a price. When we deplete the stores, we feel even more exhausted afterward. This helps explain Heidi's tearful breakdown.

Francine consoled Heidi. "Although it probably wasn't a great idea for you to risk your health by clearing the driveway, you proved that you can do anything, even tasks you have never tried before. Your illness probably sapped your reserves which is why you let him get to you so deeply. The worst is the loneliness, the feeling you have nowhere to turn." Francine explained that the only one who can truly make you happy is yourself. "I'm 53 and went to a movie by myself for the first time in my life, and survived. Now if I could get up the nerve to go dancing by myself!"

Taking the Controls: Positive Approaches to Anger

While anger is a normal, even useful, emotion, it can undermine emotional health as well as lead to problems at work, with friends and family, and in every other aspect of life if the person can't control it.

LaVonne was so furious at Billy that she took it out on everyone, including the children. "For a week after he told me he didn't know if he wanted to stay married, I had to have something in my mouth to bite. I found that carrots and other raw veggies helped—at least they were better than chips. I even ground my teeth when I slept and woke up with a sore jaw!"

In order to deal with anger, people suppress it, express it, or find a way to soothe themselves. To express upset in an assertive—rather than aggressive—way, the person must explain what her needs are and how they can be met without being demanding or pushy, and by respecting the other person as well as herself. Some Midlife Wives Club members, who have avoided conflict at all costs and not felt worthy of being heard, admitted difficulty in this area. Many women have trained themselves to suppress or redirect irritable feelings. If a temper can translate into a window-washing marathon, the result might be a brighter outlook as well as a cleaner home. But if the anger is not released, it may act like a ricocheted bullet that strikes back in the form of high blood pressure, headaches, or depression. Other pathological expressions of anger include:

- Passive-aggressive behavior (getting back at people indirectly, without telling them why, rather than confronting them head-on)

- Acting cynical about everything

- Being hostile inappropriately

- Putting others down

- Harsh, sarcastic humor

- Poor relationships with others

If possible, angry people should endeavor to not only control their outward behavior, but actually lower their physiological response, even their racing pulse. This is easier said than done.

Few women blow up and punch out the man who made them angry. They are more likely to sulk, withdraw, or become ill. Even women who previously have coped well with life's inevitable ups and downs feel they have been tossed into a stormy sea without a life raft when their husbands reject them. Club members offer these ideas for coping:

- Try relaxation techniques like deep breathing, imagery, and yoga.

- Reframe thoughts about him to positive images of your children or other people who make you happy.

- Don't refer to him, yourself, or anyone else with words like "always" or "never." Instead look for shades of gray.

- Remind yourself that anger hurts *you* more than him.

- Remind yourself that you are not the only one in the world with this problem.

- Read the posts online to find like-minded women with whom to share your experiences. Venting in a safe place helps!

- Realize that you *do* have a right to be angry when your life has been turned upside down and it was not your fault.

- Recognize that not every problem has an easy solution. You may be in for a long, difficult journey, but it will be easier to take baby steps and make preparations than rail at the unfairness.

- Make plans for various contingencies so you have some ideas of how you might live with and without him.

- Plan to give it your best shot—no matter what he does.

- Take care of yourself—mentally and physically.

- Take care of your children. Greet them with a smile. They can be the unwitting victims of your internal anger.

- Don't jump to the worst conclusions. In the heat of the moment, we tend to think the worst will happen.

- Use words carefully—they are hard to recall.

- Listen thoughtfully to him. It may be difficult to hear what he is saying. Does he really want to leave you or does he just need space to try out his transitioning personality?

- You may feel blamed, but don't knee-jerk too soon. What is underlying his words? Is he telling you that he is feeling neglected and unloved? What could you do to help with those feelings?

- Humor can bring perspective. Be silly, laugh, tell jokes, and try not to take everything seriously.

- Having an especially bad day? Share it with a friend or post it online. "The worst day since boot camp" stories can be fun to tell—you get both sympathy and laughs.

- While humor can put you on a constructive path, don't laugh off your problems, because that might be a form of denial.

- No one person is all right, nor is the other all wrong. Avoid taking the moral high ground and not accepting failings in others—or yourself.

- Alter your schedule so you don't feel the loss at predictable times.

- Plan some personal time for yourself, especially around events that are often stressful. The traditional "arsenic hour" before dinner finds parents and children at their worst. Prepare a protein snack (cheese, peanut butter, meat rolls) to boost blood sugar, put your feet up to read the paper, make a phone call, or check your e-mail for 30 minutes.

- Avoid alcohol or non-prescription drugs. They won't help.

- Arrange important discussions with your spouse when you are not tired. Make an appointment in the morning or at a time convenient for you.

- Don't sweat the small stuff. Does it matter if your child's bed is made or her room is clean? Close the door and walk away.

- Find less stressful alternatives in your routine like joining a car pool, taking public transportation, telecommuting one day a week, using more convenience foods.

- Discuss out-of-control feelings with a professional counselor.

- Learn more about being assertive to find positive ways to get your needs met and be less frustrated.

- Use the hints in *You Can't Say That to Me: Stopping the Pain of Verbal Abuse—An 8 Step Program* and *The Gentle Art of Verbal Self-Defense* by Suzette Haden Elgin.

Just as we cannot change what is happening with a midlife man, we cannot change the fact that life will always be filled with disappointment, pain, loss, and the unpredictable actions of others. However, we can alter the way we permit unforeseen events to affect us. As Buddha said, "Holding on to anger is like grasping a hot coal with the intent of throwing it at someone else; you are the one getting burned." So, if a woman learns productive ways to manage her responses, she will have found one of the keys to long-term happiness.

First Aid Station

"I've finally hit the bottom," posted Heidi in the middle of one lonesome Texas night. "After 30 years, Jack has abandoned us completely. Earlier this evening I left him a tearful voice mail. He called back to ask what was wrong. I blurted, 'How could you do this to me?' which infuriated him. He said he would stop by tomorrow 'to discuss the terms of our divorce.' How will I get through that? I know he'll rip out my heart, stomp on it, and kick it aside. Is there any way to protect myself?"

Darcy, who had logged on from halfway around the world, responded in minutes. "Six months ago I felt that the pain would never get better, yet today I enjoy parts of my life. It isn't great, but the despair is no longer as overwhelming."

Katie jumped in with some practical pointers. "Heidi, take a deep breath. Let it out. Now take another deep breath. Let it out. Keep on breathing deeply. Do this while you are reading online and every time you feel that wave of panic. It works. You *will* get out of this pit. The only way is up. Here's a list of what to try, one baby step at a time:

- Reach out to friends and let them hold you. Let them help you carry this heavy burden.

- See your doctor and tell him what is going on in your life.

- Consider medications. You may need help sleeping more soundly. You won't want to be on these drugs forever, but they can help during the acute phase. If you sleep better, you'll function better. If you function better, you'll make better choices.

- Find a counselor. You need a professional local support person.

- Get a lawyer, if you don't already have one. Don't agree to any divorce terms without legal advice.

- Consider a mediator, even early in the process. This is a way for you to develop solutions that serve you and your family best.

- Plan to chat online with us every evening. Unload your problems of the day here. We don't get tired of listening and we want to hear how you are doing. We know the hell you are going through, and someone is always willing to lend a sympathetic ear and offer comfort."

Inez felt like she was listening to her twin. "We are in the same boat, Heidi. On our twenty-ninth anniversary last year, Diego took me to dinner. Then we went to our cabin on the lake and made love. On the way home, he gave me 'the speech.' I'm 51 and alone, and he's having a fling with a girl half his age. I thought about killing myself, but then someone in the club told me that even though you are in the dark pit, nobody is going to save you but yourself. So dig with your fingers until you see a shaft of light. First, I had to find a reason to live that day. Don't laugh, but when I first asked myself that question, I realized that if I died, nobody would feed or walk the dog! So, for the sake of the dog I found a bit of light. From there, I was motivated for my children. I wanted them to see how an adult handles unfairness. Then there are my parents, who are in their eighties. They need me too. The reality is that your husband doesn't love you any longer and is not coming home. I know that is harsh, but it is the truth. Now, start digging. You will find your personal reasons for living. Cling to them."

Rest Area: Turning to Friends

Recent studies suggest women have an alternate defense against stress besides fight or flight: They turn to each other. This is hardly a shock to Midlife Wives Club members, who not only fill emotional needs with online support, but recommend that the women in dire straits seek out female friends, family members, and local support groups. A groundbreaking UCLA study indicates that women respond to stress with a torrent of brain chemicals that propel them to form as well as preserve friendships with other women. While this may not have surprised our aunts and grandmothers, the news has upset the stress research applecart, which, not surprisingly, has primarily involved male subjects.

"Until this study was published, scientists generally believed that when people experience stress, they trigger a hormonal cascade that revs the body to either stand and fight or flee as fast as possible," explained Dr. Laura Cousino Klein, an assistant professor of biobehavioral health at Pennsylvania State University and one of the study's authors. Now it appears that when the hormone oxytocin is released as part of the stress response in a woman, it buffers the fight-or-flight response and encourages her to tend children and gather with other women instead. When she actually engages in this tending or befriending, studies suggest that more oxytocin is released, which further counters stress and produces a calming effect.

Testosterone, which increases with stress in men, acts to combat the effects of oxytocin, while estrogen acts to enhance it. So women under pressure "tend and befriend" while men "pretend and defend." This may help explain why women outlive men since reducing stress also lowers blood pressure, heart rate, and cholesterol. "There's no doubt," says Klein, "that friends are helping us live longer." The longitudinal Nurses' Health Study from Harvard Medical School found that the more friends women had, the less likely they were to develop physical impairments as they aged and the more likely they were to be leading a joyful life. In fact, the results were so significant, the researchers concluded that not having a close friend was as detrimental to health as smoking or carrying extra weight. While nobody has studied how this relates to a spouse's midlife crisis, the researchers examined how women fared after a spouse's death and learned that those women who had a close confidante were more likely to weather the experience without any new physical impairment or permanent loss of vitality. Betsy

According to researcher Dr. Ruthellen Josselson, coauthor of *Best Friends: The Pleasures and Perils of Girls' and Women's Friendships,* often our routines keep us so busy that we don't make time for female friendships. "That's really a mistake, because women are such a source of strength to each other. We nurture one another. And we need to have unpressured space in which we can do the special kind of talk that women do when they're with other women. It's a very healing experience."

Therapists don't make house calls, few friends can be called at three in the morning, siblings and other relatives are not always available, yet there is usually somebody online at the moment a sympathetic ear is needed. The Midlife Wives Club serves many functions but perhaps none more valuable than being a lifeline when anxiety overrides any attempt at perspective in the middle of the night.

When Jasmine needed words of comfort, Jenelle was quick to respond. "I remember those first few months. Weekends felt like months. You become introspective and isolated because you are processing the changes and deciding what you want your life to be like. There may come a point when your husband will want to communicate with you again. If you know what you need, you can discuss matters on a more give-and-take basis. Some endings are irrevocable. Others are more like rewrites, where the relationship is shaken up to see where the pieces are, and put back into a more loving mold."

Motion Sickness: Will Drugs Help?

Some members, like Alegra, required immediate advice. "I have to get something to help me through this. Someone suggested antidepressants. What effect do they have? Will they make me happy all the time or alleviate my loneliness? How long will it be before they take effect? I'm not dealing with this very well and I can't afford to let it ruin other parts of my life—like work."

"Your general physician can prescribe them," responded Lettie, "but mine wasn't sympathetic. My next visit was to my gynecologist—a woman—and I cried for an hour in her office (and that was *before* they found the lump in my breast!). But after listening to me, she prescribed Zoloft. She explained how it works on the brain synapses. When I got the pills, I was hesitant to take them, but figured I couldn't feel much worse than I did. They do take the edge off so you can function better. They are by no means 'happy' pills. The effect is not immediate; it took over a week to feel the improvement."

Daisy said, "Before I took Paxil, I felt out of control, like I was losing my mind, and that feeling is not entirely gone. It didn't solve my problems, but helped me to think more rationally. I had to try a few brands before I found the best one for me, and that's not uncommon. Also, my gynecologist did some blood tests and found I was beginning menopause, even though I am only 45. So I chose to start hormone replacement too. Between the two drugs I am feeling much better."

Depressive symptoms don't always strike in the first weeks or months when the man is behaving differently. Women often believe that "this too will pass" or are so caught up in their daily routine that they don't allow themselves to imagine what the future will bring. Denial and wishful thinking play a role in delaying the inevitable.

"Things have gone from bad to worse. The kids and I moved out last summer and now Norm has filed for divorce," wrote Stacey. "He's living with the other woman. I was okay until the paperwork came from the lawyers, but then I found I was sleeping through the alarm, and having difficulty handling any routine matter from grocery shopping to filing at work. The house is a mess and all I want to do is crawl in bed. I had been seeing a counselor, so I made an emergency appointment. She says I am bordering on 'severe depression' and wants me to consider medication. It is going on two years now, so I should be getting over it. Has anyone else experienced a setback or do I belong in a nuthouse?"

Kristin reached out with a cyber hug. "I could have written that post several months ago. It has been almost three years since Dan left. Recently I sold my home and moved in with my parents. I thought it would help to have their support, but when I took a nose-dive into the dark sea of depression, I stopped fighting my therapist and agreed to try an antidepressant. Now I want to kick myself for waiting so long. For the first time in several years, I feel balanced. I can't believe pills helped me let go—something that I fought for a long time—but maybe they calmed me down enough to realize I have a lot to live for."

Whether or not to take antidepressant medication is a recurrent theme with both male and female club members. Resistance to medication and therapy is common, although minds are changed through group discussion. In England, Grace struggled with the same decisions as Stacey in Indiana. "I am shocked at my level of depression, even though our divorce is final. I thought I was over Roger, so why can't I sleep? The weight is beginning to pile on and I can't face cooking or cleaning. But I don't want to pop a pill because I think that's just a way to avoid dealing with the crux of the problem. After reading about how it helped so many people in the club, though, I am tempted."

Maud was direct with her response. "Take the stuff! Would you take insulin for diabetes? Would you take seizure meds if you had epilepsy? Would you get a cast for a broken leg? Would you suffer sick headaches without a pain pill? Then why deny yourself the medicine that will put you back on the road to this recovery?"

Share the Load: Spiritual Support

Active members of a spiritual community are fortunate to have accessible pastoral help. Even though most feel reluctant to reveal their marriage woes, they soon realize that they are suffering a common ailment and most clergy are all too familiar with both male and female crisis issues.

At a low point during her marriage to Frank, when Pat was looking for a place to crash her car, she felt something turn inside her. "Even though I don't consider myself religious, I had the sensation of being cradled in strong arms and I felt more protected than I had in years. It was as if a higher power was helping me see that my life was worth living even if my husband didn't seem interested in being a part of it. That was the last I thought of suicide."

At first Annie kept going because of her sons, but then she began to believe each test is set before us for a reason. "I learned a capacity for compassion and understanding that I never had before, so I log in here to help somebody else whose soul is hurting. My faith also gave me strength to stand tall even when I felt I could barely crawl."

"I have never been a church-going person," Lee responded, "but God has always been important to me. After James left, I began praying every night for strength I needed as well as understanding. He didn't let me down."

His Turn: Ellis

"The first few months after I left home, I was trying to find the answers at the bottom of a glass of beer. One night I went out into the yard. A bright moon was dancing in and out of the clouds. I was dwelling on my problems, feeling every 'beer muscle' in my body. I started shouting, 'Why me?' and 'How could you let this happen?' and 'Just take me now, I have no reason to live.' The only sound came from howling dogs. I yelled into the blackness, 'If you're really there, answer me already!'

"No lightning struck, no clouds parted, no thundering voice made it through my drunken stupor. Then my thoughts turned to another man who, 2,000 years before, had stood in a garden and asked many of the same questions of God. He had done nothing wrong either. He also didn't understand God's plan for him. As desperate as my situation seemed to me, it paled in comparison to the agony Christ felt. That was the moment I turned the corner and started heading in the right direction again."

"My faith is being sorely tested," Tammy posted in distress. "I tried to be the angelic one, telling Kyle I understood what he was going through. Now he's moved away to live nearer the other woman. About a month ago I bought Norman Vincent Peale's *Positive Imaging*. I was riveted by Peale's quote from Mark 11:24: 'What things soever ye desire, when ye pray, believe that ye receive them, and ye shall have them.' So I started to read about how belief also needs faith to work. Last night I woke up around two so full of anxiety and sadness I fell to my knees and begged God to give me peace, bring me love, if not from Kyle, then from Him. I prayed to be free of the hurt and pain and also for all my friends in the club to find peace too. It also helped me to breathe deeply and chant: 'Let go, let go, let go.' I told myself over and over: 'I'm worthy of love.' Now I believe He *will* see me through."

Elinor said that they had little to do with their synagogue except attend services for bar mitzvahs and High Holy days, or to take the boys to religious school. "One day when I was picking up the children, I read the bulletin board. On an impulse I decided to join a woman's study group because I was going stir crazy at home. Getting back to my religious roots was comforting, but more important, those women turned out to be my lifeline during the darkest days."

"I've not only printed out club members' pertinent posts for Eugene to read," wrote Mallory when she first joined the Midlife Wives Club, "but I gave him *Men in Midlife Crisis* by Jim Conway. Finally he admitted that he was having a crisis and that he didn't know how to deal with his conflicting emotions."

Conway, a minister and psychologist who was blindsided by his midlife crisis, turned his trauma into a cottage industry to help others. His book, first published in 1978, is cited by members as one of the most useful guides. His late wife, Sally, chimed in two years later with *Your Husband's Midlife Crisis*, which looked at the situation from the woman's point of view. See the Appendix for more information about their many books relating to midlife, marriage, and divorce, which all have a Christian perspective. Sally says that "during Jim's crisis, however, I found that the determination to grit my teeth, bear the burden, turn the other cheek, and fill the air with positive thinking wasn't enough to carry me through the long, hard days—and nights. God's grace was also essential. I more than ever needed to have a good relationship with my Lord, who promised to be with me wherever I went and whatever I went through." Both Conways were surprised when their faith and church-centered lives did not inoculate them against Jim's crisis. They each worked through his subsequent passage differently, taking strength from their religion and finding wisdom in scripture.

Parking Options: Family Support

Most Midlife Wives Club members look for support among family, friends, and professional counselors. Frequent early queries on the website are about how to tell parents, co-workers, and adult and young children. Faced with conflicting advice, members wonder whose to follow. Michelle said that she wanted to rely on family and friends but later regretted venting her day-to-day experiences. "My parents were there for me with all-encompassing love and support, but guess what? It backfired when Ted and I started to talk about reconciliation. My mother and father said I'd be an idiot to take him back after what he had done."

"I needed someone who was nonjudgmental, a good listener who wasn't going to try to fight the battle for me, but it is best not to tell everyone everything," Annie said. "Because my sisters wanted to protect me, they made value judgments about Larry.

Whenever I talked about getting back together, they'd freak and tell me never to trust him again. I think I forgave him long before they did. And because I revealed some private matters, they will never respect him again." Annie explained that getting her family's support was a two-edged sword. "I don't know what I would have done without their encouragement during the three years Larry and I were separated, but he might have come home sooner if he felt he would have been accepted without so much animosity."

Annie and many others recommended the impartial help found in a peer support group or during pastoral or psychological counseling. Many women are willing to seek help, but since they did not originate the problem, they want their spouses to join them in the hopes that they can patch up their marriage.

"I did a lot of reading," offered LaVonne, "and realized that all men go through psychological passages as they age. Most transition smoothly, but Billy wasn't that fortunate. He was sleeping poorly and dragging himself to work. I showed him some of the books and mentioned that he might benefit from counseling. Indignantly he brushed them aside. So I marked some sections with sticky tabs and asked that he just skim those pages. I knew he would see himself, even hear some of the same words he had been using. But I didn't bug him. A week later I gave him a piece of a paper with the names of three psychologists and wrote in parentheses which one was recommended by our family doctor and which by our pastor. There was also the name of a psychiatrist who could prescribe antidepressants. I doubted he would choose him, but that's the one he did end up seeing! When Billy realized he had depressive symptoms that could be medicated without months of talking sessions, he sought help."

Other men are more reluctant. "Counseling was out of the question for Eugene," wrote Mallory. "He tried it a few times after he met the other woman and said he didn't like being psychoanalyzed. I think the visits were getting tougher and he bolted before he had to confront any serious issues."

His Turn: Harrison

"The most important reason for going to a shrink is to gain insight. You should learn:

1. How you feel by discussing what has gone on in your life that brought you there and how you felt when it happened.

2. Why you feel that way. This may involve talking about your life experiences. Usually you delve into your childhood and work your way back to where you are now and see if there are any patterns.

3. What you might do to avoid the unhealthy habits that might be causing the intense stress.

4. Techniques to relieve the symptoms including exercise, diet, or medication."

Melody said she developed a community of three close friends for support. "However, I went to counseling for third-party input. My therapist puts a professional spin on the subject and she challenged me to rethink how I might have contributed to the problems. For instance, I used to let Floyd walk all over me. Now I'm learning to walk away from him when he's having one of his black moods."

Megan said, "My shrink put me on anti-anxiety meds for the panic attacks because, as he said, 'I can't work on you if I can't find you.' He compared me to a horse and a rider: the horse being the emotion, and the rider being the intellect. While the rider is on the horse holding the reins, she trots peacefully through life. But if the rider gets thrown, the horse goes into flight mode, gallops off blindly, stumbling, falling, picking itself up, and galloping some more. With a lot of work, as well as help from this guy, I have reached the stage during which I can curtail the emotional flight and let the intellect take over. But I know that this is not something I would have achieved without the insight I received from him."

Jenelle said, "You know when you have the right therapist because it is someone who is on your wavelength. Different strokes—literally—for different folks. It should be someone you trust, somewhere you feel safe, someone comforting—or challenging. You set the criteria that you think will work best for your personality. You should feel better—not worse—after the visit and you should feel you are making progress, even if it is baby steps."

Shock Absorbers

"Rollercoaster ride," "bumpy road," and "rough journey" are a few of the most common phrases Midlife Wives Club members use to describe the emotional upheavals their midlife men set in motion. When a woman recognizes she is dealing with a creature that she cannot corral, she begins to ponder how to proceed—with him or without him. Club members complain that the old signals are blurred and just as they think they understand what course to take, another roadblock appears.

Eileen was in a quandary. "I don't know what to think. In early December Chester announced he was leaving right after Christmas. So I prepared for that, but he never left. Same thing in January, but he's still here. Nothing is resolved and I hate living with the tension that he might walk out tomorrow. Sometimes I almost wish he would do it, but I don't want to lose him and I don't want to be the one to throw him out. Last month he said, 'However this ends up, I don't regret any part of our life together.' Yesterday he complained, 'I've let you control me for too long.' Then today he called from work and said, 'Wish we could start over and be like we were when we were dating.' Is he messing with my head?"

"Hans said the same things!" wrote Jette from The Netherlands. "I think it is a power play. The more they shake you up, the more control they have. The last time Hans said he wanted a divorce, I responded, 'Okay, if that is what you want, I won't stop you,' and walked away. Three days later he came to me and said, 'I don't think divorce is the answer.' Now he's on a trip to France to think about his options."

Mimi posted, "Quentin said some rotten things to me, but I realized that he could only feel in control if he had someone to blame for his unhappiness. It also helped him justify leaving a relationship that was not broken. The turning point came when I realized that I was not responsible for his happiness and he was not responsible for mine either. I'm finding ways to keep myself busy without him—just in case. The best medicine is to detach as much as you can and take care of yourself."

"If you want to change the dynamics of the situation, create a game that you can win, which is easier said than done," Jocelyn suggested. "I'm an actress and if someone criticized my performance, I blew it off as their opinion because only I knew if I had done my best. But, when Marshall rejected me, it was an unexpected blow because I believed I was safe in my own home. I punched pillows. I yelled and screamed in the dark. I ruined a newly painted wall by splattering it with another color."

After Bettina poured out her latest problems with Dimitri,

she confessed to the club, "I met a cool guy through work yesterday and he invited me for a drink. What a great boost to my ego! I don't know if I'm supposed to be doing that if I want to fix my marriage—which I do—but it helped to have someone telling me I was beautiful."

Harriet was quick with advice for Bettina. "You have been rejected and are not thinking clearly. If you're not careful, you will be drawn into an affair, which will only make matters worse because you will feel guilty. I almost fell for one guy, but now I am happy that I stayed clear of temptation while Yves was in the depths of his midlife crisis. Two wrongs don't make anything right. Maybe the flattery and the fact that your wiring was lit up will help you understand how he might have been tempted by someone else. Use this insight to save your marriage, if you can."

Keys to Inner Peace

When Claudette asked Herman to sign a document and get it notarized, he was rude. "Lately he treats me as if I'm the one who cheated on him and left him with a bunch of bills. How can I put an end to him jerking me around with his unkindness? Everyone says I have to play the cards I've been dealt, but what if the deck has been stacked against me or he's taken all the high cards?"

Lee reminded Claudette of a Midlife Wives Club mantra: "His behavior does not determine my worth."

Betty agreed. "All the answers lie within you. You have to find personal fulfillment alone, not with another person. Once you find the keys to do that, you may realize that you don't need the other person as much as you thought you did. In fact, it may have been a habit to have him around. For a long time Jonathan and I were like roommates. Now that he is gone, I feel liberated. No more walking on eggshells, no more trying to do anything and everything to please him. This is my situation. Everyone has to decide what parts to keep, what to rebuild, and what to discard."

"Do they one day wake up and say, 'Oh, I really do love you,' and kiss and make up?" asked Maura. "Sleeping next to each other night after night with no intimacy is tough, but he hasn't left home, so I hope he'll recover, like he's been in some sort of trance."

Francine said she was living in the same limbo as Maura. "Martin doesn't speak to me unless I initiate the conversation. When I pressed him, he said he doesn't hate me; he just has no feelings for me—and that's after six children and 25 years together. He's having an affair with a 28-year-old woman in his office, but still living at home. I feel like I am the greatest failure on earth. My self-esteem has always been wrapped up in him and how I see myself reflected in his eyes. I have been the giver, and in a quiet, manipulative way he's the taker. The rejection and sense of abandonment, not to mention the insecurity of knowing the trust will never be the same, are what hurt the most. I didn't know where to begin, but I decided I had to do something for myself besides lying in bed and hoping to die. So I joined the Y and started working out, which made me feel better. Hey, I couldn't feel *worse*! I am a little bit stronger every day and now I am starting to think I could live without him."

Marina encouraged Francine. "Yesterday my 9-year-old son was down because he was having trouble with friends at school. I told him, 'You have to love yourself if you want people to love you, and the best way to make friends is to be friendly.' Then I explained that I hadn't loved myself very much, but that now I did. He's so sharp that he replied, 'If that is true, then maybe now Dad will love you again and won't leave.' I told him if his dad did love me again, that would be great, but if he couldn't, that would be okay too because I now loved myself. He threw his arms around me and said that he is going to try and love himself, too. Then, last night I forced myself to go to a party alone. Everyone came up to me and said how great I looked. One girl remarked that I seemed so sure and confident and asked if I'd been on vacation. I laughed and told her about my little journey. She said 'Congratulations,' and added, 'Normally I wouldn't say that to someone on the verge of a divorce, but it seems appropriate because you look like you are going to do fine.' So, if someone is packing your bags for you, go on the journey. I hope it works out as well as mine has so far."

Midlife Wives Club members keep reminding each other that the changes in their lives have set them on a journey—an unplanned one, a scary one, even a dangerous one. Nobody has a road map or knows what is around the next bend. Most never wanted to go on the trip in the first place. For most it is a forced march at first. Some are dragged along by the spouses even though they were happy at home. But then they mention that they are seeing amazing new sights—really insights into themselves—and decide it is the trip of a lifetime.

CHAPTER 9

Forks in the Road: Picking the Best Option

Life is its own journey, presupposes its own change and movement, and one tries to arrest them at one's eternal peril.

—Laurens van der Post, written in 1951, age 45

"Not all midlife marriage problems are a midlife crisis, but some are," Annie responded to a panicky newcomer. Researchers also have determined that only a small fraction of midlife issues ever reach the crisis stage. In *The Perilous Bridge: Helping Clients Through Midlife Transition,* social crisis expert Naomi Golan writes that a stressful situation becomes a crisis when there is a convergence of the normal changes in midlife transition with one of two types of crisis. One is the *shock crisis*—a sudden, often unexpected event such as the death of someone close—which may cause a release of emotions that overwhelms the normal coping mechanisms. The other is the *exhaustion crisis,* which builds slowly as various difficult events—the children leaving home, job difficulties, medical issues—pile up until the person reaches his breaking point. "In either case, disequilibrium and active crisis results," writes Golan.

Annie's practical experience reinforces the theoretical. "In the beginning it's hard to figure out what is going on. It is essential to get a grip because you have a lot to lose by acting out of desperation. Emotions are not calls to action; they are merely feelings. Happily most midlife crises are temporary. In the meantime I recommend patience, faith, detachment, humor, support, and prayer, if you are so inclined."

Lost in Space: Men's Confused Emotions

The man in crisis is an emotional basket case—even if he doesn't realize it. Women are more likely to own up to feeling forlorn and confused. "Dan's emotions seem out of control," Kristin told the group. "Last night he called from his new house crying and asked if I needed anything. He said he'd been looking at old photos and was overcome with sorrow about what he was losing. When I checked on him today, he talked about recycling the old paint in the basement. All the emotion was gone. How do men do that? At times I wish I could!"

His Turn: Harrison

"For the first time since childhood I find myself in tears. I was taught that 'big boys don't cry' but all that did was force me to avoid feelings, and that has been a recipe for disaster later in life. Until now I handled my emotions by ignoring them, burying them, or blaming someone else. I know this phase is a result of my depression. I used to appear cold in order to bury the feelings, but now that I realize there is something wrong with me, maybe I will be more open and improve."

Dr. Alon Gratch, who believes that much of men's anger and confusion stems from male insecurity, explains that many therapists see the "dynamic of the angry, critical, or explosive husband with the wounded, tearful, and defeated wife." Gratch says that the man's aggression intimidates his "opponent," catches her off guard, violates her psychic—if not her physical—space in order to penetrate it, occupy it, and create a wall of bitterness that will psychologically separate him from her. He explains, "We can clearly see traces of a man's fear of losing himself in a woman."

Balancing Acts: Setting Boundaries

During the entire crisis period, the wife feels destabilized. She may keep shifting her stance and wondering what she could try to bring him back, or maybe it is time to push him away entirely and travel on with her life. Only the woman herself can set the bar for what she will accept, how much she will sacrifice, what the marriage is worth, and whether she is better off with or without him. Sometimes the choice is made for her; other times she is able to make the final move.

When the other woman blurs the picture, one of the first decisions is whether or not to confront him or wait it out. Colleen admitted it took a while before she had the courage to challenge Rory, and even when she did, he deceived her by saying he wasn't "seeing anyone." By then Colleen knew the other woman was in another country for a while. "One night we were in a bar and a few drinks gave me the nerve to call him on the semantics. When Rory told her I knew, she was so ashamed she wanted to break up with him. As a result, I became the bad guy for discovering what he was doing!"

"My doctor, who was treating me for weight loss connected

with the stress of Baker's actions, advised me to get a lawyer long before I thought it necessary," wrote Dorathea. "Baker was acting weirdly, especially about money. I had to protect myself and the children. While I still hope we can work it out, the meeting with the attorney was confidential, and I feel better knowing my rights."

Whenever midlife mayhem occurs, it spills over into the person's relationship with their spouse. Golan suggests that some of this disruption is due to the conflicts that arise during these transitional years as well as the shifting nature of the marriage itself. Other tensions may be reactive to or are the consequences of changes in other facets of the midlife situation—like health or job problems—or to unexpected external pressures. "Whatever the source of the disturbance, it frequently becomes played out in the marital area," Golan explains. The married couple's primary task at this stage is *rediscovery* versus *despair*. According to Golan, "The durability of the marriage depends on the adaptations made to reestablish a satisfactory balance between the spouses."

Just at the point they are threatened with being abandoned, many Midlife Wives Club members are advised to give their husbands "space," which is easier said than done. Winona explained that Bud signed a six-month lease on an apartment because he needed "time out to sow wild oats" and to find out if he had missed anything by marrying his first love. He told her, "I need the freedom to come and go without permission and maybe I can get whatever is bugging me out of my system." Bud acknowledged that he might sleep with other women, but would come home when the lease was up. "I'm worried about sexually transmitted diseases or an unplanned pregnancy, but he denies that could ever happen to *him*. Bud thinks I should be satisfied if he willingly returns, but he can't waltz into my life any time he feels like it unless he agrees to work on our marriage."

Evie advised Winona to look after herself and her daughter. "While Bud's out in 'space,' you need to plant your feet on the ground and progress toward independence. That doesn't preclude keeping the door open by invitation only and communicating regularly. If he ever does come home, he will find you a more complete person and everyone will benefit." Evie also said that Winona did not have to condone Bud's sleeping around. "Tell him how you feel about his actions, and while you still love him, you strongly disapprove of what he is doing."

"I left Hal alone as much as possible," Jenelle explained. "I made no major demands, didn't subject him to any deep relationship talks. This removed the pressure and helped him realize that the problem was within. He also didn't have to move out to come to terms with what he wanted."

"I tried to be understanding," Mavis replied to this discussion, "and Eric stayed home. We shared the same bed, hugged, kissed, held hands, snuggled at night, and even had lukewarm sex once in a while. He continued to bring me coffee in the morning, and we shared some activities like meals out. We also started counseling. So what's wrong with this picture? Last week Eric told me he found an apartment and is moving during the middle of the month!"

Yolanda was sympathetic. "Whether you like it or not, you have no control over what happens in his life, but that doesn't mean you don't have complete control of your own. Your husband is lost, frightened, and bewildered, and you are too. The good news is that—for today—he's still with you and you're communicating. In counseling maybe you can discuss why he is moving and what his goal might be."

"You can set some of your own goals too," Winona suggested. "Make a list of things you have wanted to do but didn't interest him. Go to plays or museums. Rent the videos you prefer. When Bud announced he was moving, I told him that I was going to get rid of some ugly carpeting, reorganize the kitchen, move the dining room table, and rearrange the living room. He started to complain, then I told him that he could do what he wanted with his new place—but this would now be *my* space. That took some of the wind out of his sails!"

Annie added that while some of the befuddled men keep their problems to themselves, they usually look to an outsider for comfort. "If you can get to the man before another woman does, then there is hope that love won't be forever lost."

Club members report difficulty in fielding unexpected volleys of anger that are directed at them for no obvious reason. Corinne said, "When Monroe and I discussed our plans, he turned vicious. An hour after the outburst, I came downstairs to find him back to normal. He was like a real Dr. Jekyll and Mr. Hyde. I try to appease him because if I make him mad, he can cut off our money."

Lorraine jumped in. "You must keep telling yourself this is not your fault! He is projecting his anger, his guilt, his unhappiness onto you. If you argue with him, he will justify leaving you. If you don't respond, he won't have nourishment to feed his frenzy. If you apologize to keep the peace, that further validates his actions because you are admitting you did something wrong. So you have to maintain your composure, refuse to give in to his rage as well as refuse to accept his words as the truth. You can't repair the past so don't fall into the 'if only' trap; and you can't predict the future so avoid the 'what if' pit as well."

Club members joined in a chorus to encourage Corinne to get legal advice because she was vulnerable financially. "When a man is thinking primarily about *his* feelings, *his* needs, it is likely that many of hers will be sacrificed," Jasmine reminded.

"You have to make contingency plans. If this ends up in divorce, you might get some spousal support, but probably not for life. Now's the time to get additional training, take some classes, or at least have some ideas about how you'll make it on your own. Don't wait until you have a deadline or the money dries up. Few women end up better financially after a divorce." (The Appendix offers many divorce resources including books and online and local support groups.)

His Turn: Harrison

"During my crisis I tried to upset my wife so she'd feel mad instead of sad and rejected. Also I wanted her to kick me out so I wouldn't have to take the full responsibility for leaving her. If I provoked her into doing something nasty, then I'd have something to blame her for—not that I understood this on a conscious level."

Direction Finding: Keys to Communication

Moses probably wandered in the desert for 40 years because he refused to ask for directions. Men in the midst of crisis are not inclined to follow prescriptions that might alleviate their uncertainty. Club members have tried talking to their mates, giving them books and articles to read, or suggesting counseling only to meet fierce resistance. Theologian Paul Tillich wrote, "The first duty of love is to listen." The first duty of listening is silence. Talking *to* a person is different than talking *with* someone. Just as the man may not be hearing what the wife is saying, she may not recognize his verbal or nonverbal signals. A marital rift is like a bombshell setting off a noisy clatter in the mind. As one person is speaking, the other's distressed emotions may be jamming the internal airwaves as previous slights and hurtful words are remembered. Often one person is planning their rebuttal instead of concentrating on the other's point of view. Couples in crisis have mastered "tuning out," delivering cutting comments, and having arguments on the tip of the tongue.

Cathy and Dr. Steve Brody, marital counselors and authors of *Renew Your Marriage at Midlife*, call blocks to listening "stoppers," which they divide into three categories: altruistic, analytic, and aggressive.

Altruistic stoppers include:

- Advising ("You're acting that way because that's what your father did.")

- Reassuring ("You'll feel better after a good night's sleep.")

- Denying ("You're making a big deal out of nothing.")

Analytic stoppers include:

- Lecturing ("If you'd do what this book suggests you'd be fine.")

- Judging ("You're not behaving properly.")

- Interpreting ("Your symptoms are typical of men your age.")

- Probing ("Why are you acting like this now?")

Aggressive stoppers include:

- Ordering ("Shut up and leave me alone.")

- Warning ("If you don't like it, I'm moving out.")

- Blaming ("If you hadn't done X or Y, this would never have happened.")

- Name calling ("You've always been a witch like your mother.")

One of the easiest ways to promote communication is to clear the mind of all the static, be open to the other person's thoughts, and listen quietly. Silence does not have to be filled. If each person acts interested, maintains eye contact, and ignores distractions like the TV and telephone, each will realize the other person is interested in what is being said. If the conversation falters, the listener can nod or use fillers such as "I see," "right," "yeah," or "that's news" to demonstrate continued interest.

Many women complain that their husbands don't like to talk about feelings, but an invitation to discuss what is happening coupled with a sincere attempt to listen patiently can yield results. Most people think faster than they speak, and it may take a while for him to find the right words. Many a conversation is truncated because one person cuts the other off in midthought. Some of what is heard may be painful, but if a wife wants to know what's on her husband's mind, she has to listen respectfully—not condemn his ideas or actions—and respect his right to have and express his opinions—even if they are not what she wants to hear.

Don't forget to watch for nonverbal messages. Tone of voice, facial expression, body posture, energy level, and general affect may tell more than the actual words. Comments that reflect comprehension also promote more information. "Sounds like work has been stressful" or "I guess you've been more worried about your health than I realized" are nonjudgmental and prove that the person is listening. Everything doesn't have to be said in one session. When the man seems to stare into space, starts to tell jokes, or seems teary or weary, let him off the hook. Don't turn every conversation into a tortuous experience.

Most Midlife Wives Club members report that communication has broken down and often need a third party to sort out the destructive patterns that are making meaningful dialogue impossible. "Get counseling!" is the most common advice offered, and many members extol the benefits of going as a couple. More often than not, the wife says her husband is not interested.

When Monroe refused to join her, Corinne finally went to see a therapist alone. "It gave me a chance to review the part I played, and helped me tune in to my inner voice, which I had been shutting out."

According to Polly, "Counselors don't come in one-size-fits-all. Select one with a compatible value system. After we separated, Fred and I preferred individual counseling combined with joint sessions. We used a husband/wife team and alternated weeks together and separate. At first we'd come out of some sessions worse than we went in, but eventually we got back on track."

His Turn: Brady

"Nobody else could help me find my way out of the forest when the birds ate all the crumbs. First, I examined my past to understand why I was who I was. Next, I looked to my future—which seemed to have disappeared when the crisis descended—and tried to figure out what sort of man I wanted to be. Then I worked to change what I didn't like. This process took more than a year, and I did it myself without any help from a shrink or my family."

Out in the Cold: Deciding to Stay or Go

A man may choose to leave home or remain with his family, expecting his wife to wait patiently as he sorts out his options. Not all women are that tolerant. Some club members were so devastated by their husbands' disloyalty they slammed the door in his face.

Flo divorced Rodney six weeks after finding out about his affair. "When he told me he loved her, I gave him his freedom rather than getting down on my knees. I wonder what would have happened if I had not given up so fast. I'm not the type who compromises, but now that I see he had a pattern of failed relationships and may have been depressed, I may have been too hasty."

Mallory asked for help with Eugene, who met another woman while fleeing the Twin Towers terror. "He's still in contact with the other woman, but he's living at home acting as though this is 'normal.' Meanwhile I've lost so much weight I'm a walking skeleton and I'm going to counseling alone. I can only do so much since the source of my anxiety is his denial. By letting him stay, aren't I compromising my values? Should I ask him to leave?"

Members were sympathetic to Mallory's situation. Many of their husbands had succumbed after a death in their family or other personal upheaval. "No matter what brings it on, they end up in the same boat," Enid commented. "If he remains in the house, you have a better chance because if you kick him out, he will head straight for that needy other woman."

Is divorce the answer? Does reconciliation work? What is best for the children? A controversial recent study indicates toughing it out may lead to more long-term happiness than divorce. The report, headed by Linda Waite, a sociologist at the

University of Chicago, looked at data from the National Survey of Families and Households on 5,232 married adults including 645 who said their marriages were unhappy. Within five years, 167 of the unhappy couples were divorced or separated. Of the unhappy partners who divorced, about half were happy five years later, but the unhappy spouses who stuck it out often did better. About two-thirds were happy five years later, and the biggest turnarounds came with those who had originally been the most discontented.

Three factors helped turn the tide:

- Marital endurance: job situations improved, children matured, or chronic problems came into perspective.

- Marital work: spouses actively endeavored to solve problems, change behavior, or improve communication.

- Personal change: partners found alternative ways to improve their own happiness and build a better life despite a mediocre marriage. In effect, the unhappy partner changed.

Interestingly, those who worked on their marriages rarely turned to professionals. When they did, they often went to faith-based counselors committed to helping solve marital problems. Men, particularly, were "very suspicious of anyone who wanted money to solve personal problems," according to Waite. Those who remained married generally disapproved of divorce, citing concerns about children, religious beliefs, and a fear that divorce would bring its own set of problems. Waite said, "If you compare people who were unhappy with their marriage who stayed married and people who were unhappy with their marriage and got divorced, basically you don't improve your emotional well-being on average by divorcing. It's about the same as it is for staying in an unhappy marriage, which, by the way, doesn't tend to stay unhappy." She also says that those who divorce and remarry report happiness about the same as the people who stayed married.

However, Dr. Pepper Schwartz, author of *Everything You Know about Love and Sex Is Wrong*, disputes the study's design. "I know this data set because I've worked with it. They've put divorced and separated people together. Separated people are notoriously the least happy of all. They're in transition. So, if you take the separated people out of their data, only look at the divorced people, you find, indeed, that divorced people are happier than the people who stayed in the unhappy marriage." The study also revealed that five years later there was still a high level of depression and in some cases, drinking. Schwartz says, "Depression is not necessarily responsive to either a good or bad marriage. So they were that way and they stayed that way."

Waite says, "It's true, people who are unhappy with their marriage show higher levels of depressive symptoms, but their depressive symptoms don't get better when they get divorced, even if they get remarried."

Schwartz reports that second marriages tend to be happier than first marriages: "Not necessarily more stable, but happier."

The majority of club members select a wait-and-see approach, if only by default. Some are determined to hang on by the skin of their teeth, while others either set boundaries or dig in for the long haul. Jenelle said, "For my sanity I set a date to decide whether we would continue on as a couple or not, but I did not share it with him. That way I knew my suffering in limbo had a time limit."

"Ted talked about leaving for a year, and I felt it was a form of mental cruelty because he held it over my head like a sword," Michelle admitted. "I tried to be understanding. I got angry. I detached. I stayed away from him. I built new bridges. He wouldn't go to counseling. He wouldn't give up the other woman. He wouldn't acknowledge he was depressed. Privately, I drew a line in the sand: If it wasn't better after a year, then he would have to go. When the date came, I said, 'Here's the money for your first and last month's rent.' It was the best thing I ever did because I finally could exhale."

Keeping Home Fires Burning: Ways Women Wait It Out

Many women believe that control was removed from them when their mates began to change. Some try to be understanding; others cannot tolerate the upheavals. Most find it impossible to play second fiddle to another woman. While a man may be doing everything to push his wife away—at least on the surface—he may be terrified that she will leave him.

Annie explained, "There is a 'moving-out trap' because if you don't set limits and deadlines, you are a doormat. If you do, it may validate his plan so if you later express any hurt or anger, he'll feel justified saying, 'Why are you upset? We talked about this and you agreed to it, too.' " Annie said a man must accept his decisions without making his wife the scapegoat. "Each spouse must be accountable to the other for what they do, so he has to have an explanation for his choices. If you don't like what you hear, say so and tell him why. Although there is little we can do about our spouses' actions, we are in complete charge of how we react to them."

His Turn: Harper

"Don't push him out if he's depressed. You wouldn't do it if he had a broken leg. But remember a midlife depression can last several years. If he refuses to see a doctor or counselor and is making your life miserable, you can set that as one of your conditions. You can also feel justified in asking him to leave if there's another woman and he won't give her up or if he is in any way abusive to you or the children.

"Set your personal boundaries and hold to them. That way you can take care of yourself so if or when he does come up for air, you won't be so burned out that you can't consider a reconciliation.

"Try to avoid heavy relationship discussions or pressuring him for a commitment because his inability to deal with these is part of his condition. Each man has different releases for these pressures like hiding, running, raging, and dating. If you loosen the clamps, he won't feel he needs freedom quite so badly.

"Show him you are listening to his needs. Ask about one item he would like to see improved that would make him happier in the interim, then brainstorm on how to accomplish it (more time to himself, a quieter house, getting the finances under control). This doesn't mean if that issue is better that he won't leave, but that you've made an attempt to make his life more bearable, which will set a tone that may help him heal.

"Also give back more decision-making to him. In my marriage we started to do almost everything jointly like buying a car or picking a school for our children, but it became a habit and I started to think I needed her permission for everything, which was not healthy for me."

While many men in crisis choose to leave home to work on their problems in a new environment, to experiment sexually, or to carry on a love affair, many struggle while living in the same domestic situation. This may be because they desire to save their marriage and create a better relationship, they have no other place to go, or they lack the economic resources to support two homes. Many club members ponder how to live with this disgruntled gorilla and still retain their equilibrium.

Dottie's husband, Lance, never left home. "We've battled for almost five years, but there's been some improvement in the last few months. Three years ago an Internet romance turned into a full-blown affair. After a short hiatus when Lance was more loving toward me, he admitted he was feeling the itch again and suggested I kick him out and get on with my life. That's when I found the Midlife Wives Club." After Dottie realized Lance was acting in a typical way, she stopped taking his rejection personally. "When I became more independent, Lance began initiating sex and saying he loved me. Now he's willing to start marriage counseling. Even though we both feel we will make it this time, we want the best relationship we can have and realize it will be a work in progress forever."

Although they went through rough times, several members were glad they stayed on board through the stormiest seas. "I refused to argue with Dimitri," explained Bettina. "I agreed to disagree and told him I loved him no matter what he did, even if I could not condone his actions. My marriage vows had said 'for better or *worse*,' so I chalked this up to the *worst* and stuck with him. Slowly there has been improvement. This has taught me what I am made of—so I feel better about myself too."

"Does anybody besides me truly believe that their marriage is worth trying to save?" Jade inquired. "After Boris moved out, he asked me to keep it a secret, but eventually I confided in my sister. Now she wants me to get a legal separation, but I want to save this marriage and think the best way to do it is to wait it out. Does anybody else feel this way? Or am I crazy?"

While many club members suggested it would be foolish not to get legal advice—just in case—Pauline agreed with Jade. "I've decided that after 20 years—some wonderful, some difficult—of marriage, I am not giving in. We lost two babies and endured the uncertainty of an independent adoption. All of that brought us closer, or so I thought. While I devoted myself to our child and home, Samuel was working longer hours. Eventually I learned he was having an affair with his assistant. After I got over my shock, I admitted I had neglected him in favor of our long-awaited child. So I told him I would forgive him if he would break all contact and go into counseling with me. It worked—for a while. We moved into a new home for a fresh start. For two years everything was fine, and then—bam!—he needed his space, said life is too short, all the usual midlife ravings. Most people think this is the moment to throw in the towel, but I got through the first storm, and believe this one will pass as well. Our child needs both of us, so I'm keeping the porch light on until he comes to his senses—again."

Should you let him stay home but allow him to behave as if he isn't married? Should you encourage him to try his wings and hope he'll come crawling back? Do separations work? Many Midlife Wives Club members advocate working on the agreements recommended in *Should I Stay or Go? How Controlled Separation Can Save Your Marriage* by Lee Raffel.

Colleen said they used the book to organize how they would separate. "It was an informal promise about how each of us would conduct ourselves and dealt with everything from finances, to who we would tell, to dating each other as well as other people." Colleen and Rory agreed to have dinner once a week, which was awkward at first. "We sometimes ended up back at my apartment, and if I wanted, he would spend the night. I never went to his place because I couldn't bear to be in that tiny room where he had taken other women." After four months Rory asked to come back, volunteered to stop seeing the other woman, and recommitted to their marriage.

Polly and Fred signed a similar document. "We are living together some of the time, but not in a normal married situation. Fred is pursuing his personal growth, and I can support him in that. In the meantime, I'm developing my interests and learning to be more self-sufficient. To me, the most important part is a time limit when we will renegotiate what to do next."

Annie warned club members not to allow their husbands to treat them like buddies or to think they can come and go through a revolving door. "If you do, one day you will hear him say, 'She was a great gal. I still miss her because this woman (his next wife) won't let me get away with that bull.' "

When Mallory brought up the idea of a separation, Eugene realized it was the eleventh hour. For the first time in months, he came up behind her and enfolded her in a bear hug. She pushed him away and told him she needed answers. "We had our first heart-to-heart since his experience with the Twin Towers tragedy. I told him how his actions had been upsetting me, and he described problems he had been having with me. I accepted responsibility for putting the children or other concerns of mine first." They agreed to think about what each had said and how they could solve their mutual problems. "That's the first 'fight' we had fair and square with everything out on the table. A small step, but one I am grateful we took together."

Buffer Zone: When Family and Friends Get Involved

Parents and extended family usually get enmeshed in the crisis—first by offering support to the wounded spouse and later by advising on how to proceed. Many club members fret over reunification issues while trying to appease indignant relatives.

"After keeping our marital tiff a secret for two years, my family finally found out about it and were furious with Boris for hurting me," Jade admitted. "Our marriage was improving, but they were interfering by being uncivil to him."

Mavis said that Eric may have stayed away longer than he would have because of his shame in front of her family. "It was my job to set them straight and I told them that while I appreciated their support, he was only responsible to me. I told my family—as well as Eric—that I would suffer whatever was necessary to bring him home because I'd never be the one to end the marriage."

The flip side of relatives is dealing with *his* family. "Dimitri's sister tried to blame me for his actions!" Bettina complained. "According to her, if he went looking for another woman, it was because there was something wrong with me. Instead of arguing, I let her know this was a private matter and closed the subject."

Astrid revealed the most egregious way relatives sabotaged a reunion. "I thought we were making progress," Astrid wrote, "then I found out that Brendan asked someone new for a date. Guess who? My sister! Even worse, my mother thinks it is okay. I must be worthless if my own sister and mother think this is appropriate. I feel the end is near. Good-bye and thanks everyone."

"That takes the cake!" Megan exclaimed. "I thought I had

won the loser lottery when George dated my (former) best friend. You're the only sane one. The rest of them need serious help."

Shana picked up on Astrid's desperation. "Astrid, are you considering suicide? When the pain was unbearable, I tried, but all it did was hurt my children worse. I still wonder why Yuri can't love me the way he did, but I know—as you must—that he is the one with the real problems. Your sister and your husband are two selfish creeps. Take back your life and be the wonderful person you are. And check in here soon because we all care!"

Astrid relieved the members of the club when she came back online. "I've come to grips with the fact that this is another form of Brendan's abuse. Since I'm not about to go on *Jerry Springer* with this story, I've moved elsewhere and will now only see him in court. I have an illness that prevents me from working, and he hasn't paid for my medication since he left. Last week he canceled my health insurance. This week he's dating my sister. Get the picture? A lawyer is working on this for me now."

Homeward Bound: When to Let Him Come Home

The husband may have moved out literally or figuratively, but after he has tested his midlife wings, he may be finding them sore and creaky. Just as a 40-year-old may have to hold a book farther away to read the fine print, he may have to view his home from a distance before he can focus on what he has left behind. Midlife Wives Club members struggle with whether they should open their doors—and hearts—again if he wants to come home.

His Turn: Judd

"I have managed to screw up everything that is important to me. I walked away from my wife, three wonderful children, and our perfect home. After I had an accident, I suffered post-traumatic stress disorder and couldn't get my balance back. That's when I became attracted to another woman. Eventually, I talked myself into leaving because I needed time to clear my head. My wife said if I went through with my plan, I'd have all the time in the world because she wouldn't be there when I came back. But I didn't listen.

"The pain of her rejection caused me to drink more in a month than ever before in my life. I got my own place and the other woman moved in. Soon I learned that everything I had done was a mistake, but the more I tried to find my way back to my wife and family, the worse it got. I want to put it all behind me and make it up to her, but I've burned every bridge and I don't know how to get to the other side."

"Troy told me that he missed being at home, and I admitted that I missed having him around too," Charlene explained. "I know he's hit rock bottom. He's broke and hanging out in bars. Should I make going to AA meetings a condition? Should I find out whether he loves me enough to work on the issues? Maybe my love for him will build him up and we'll recover what we had."

Emily counseled Charlene to put energy into solving her own problems, let Troy work on his, and see where that led. "Gabe came home three months after leaving. At first I was thrilled, but once he was back, he made it clear that he missed his house and his children, not me. Guess who had to move the next time?

Me. He wanted his creature comforts, but didn't want to change anything in our marriage."

Naomi told Charlene, "If you take him back too quickly, you may be setting yourself up for a big fall. Your husband's admission that he needs help is a step in the right direction. I'd want to see some progress with his sobriety before he came home."

"I thought Archer was coming out of it when he'd phone me to apologize, make plans for the future, wondering how he could make it up to me," Marlene added. "Face-to-face was a different story. He was home for a week before he broke all his promises. Because I changed, I had no patience for his boorish behavior. Now I am seeing an attorney."

"It's over when you've had enough!" Jenelle exclaimed. "I don't believe putting your life on hold, being at his beck and call, hoping, wishing, thinking about him, wanting to be his friend, trying to convince him that he does love you, or accepting being second best do any good. Why put up with bad behavior? Live your life! If he is meant to come back, he will."

His Turn: Harrison

"If your man is coming out of midlife crisis, he needs to answer these questions for himself—and his wife:

1. What have I learned?

2. Why am I here?

3. What do I hold dearest in my life?

4. What am I willing to do to keep those things?

5. What are my values?

If he's in the midst of a guilt trip, which happens during the course of a crisis, he may not have answers to these questions. Remember that actions speak louder than words. If you think you may want to try again, be kind, gentle, and loving, and tell him you are not ready to give up on everything wonderful you had together."

Two-way Street: Nobody's Perfect

Accepting responsibility for the damage from a midlife crisis is rough on everyone. Yes, the man may have crossed a line, but the woman probably made mistakes as well. No one person is ever one hundred percent at fault. Marriages that seemed okay may have had some hidden fissures that became huge cracks under pressure.

Francine confessed, "It took both of us to let our marriage slide to the point of infidelity. Admittedly this was the hardest pill to swallow. At first I moaned and groaned about 'poor me,' but we couldn't reconcile until I accepted my share of the blame for the breakdown of the relationship."

His Turn: Adam

"Although I made many mistakes during my crisis, I never stopped loving my wife. Every time she turned away from me in bed, put me down, or said something hateful, it drove me closer and closer to the edge. The fact that I became infatuated with a younger woman was part of the fallout. Somehow I managed to skate through my hell without throwing away my marriage. Counseling helped her see how I reacted to her angry responses, rejection, and inattention. We still have problems and I still have setbacks—sometimes severe—but at least I am getting treatment for depression. I used to be confident; the events of the last few years have taken a toll.

"I fought to hold my love for my wife. Once she realized how much pain I was in, she remained steadfast. It takes two working together to get through this."

"When Robert's crisis began we were both unsatisfied in the marriage," Evie admitted. "He was depressed so that made him gloomy and he also had some physical problems. It didn't occur to me to bail—or that he would. Before that low point, our business was flourishing, we were involved in sports with the kids, and I felt loved and appreciated. The memory of those good times kept me going through the worst moments."

Polly agreed that while in retrospect their marriage was stagnant, she had been resigned to the fact that she couldn't always be deliriously happy. "I thought we were in a trough and would bounce back. I have to accept responsibility for not realizing Fred was depressed and for not taking his misery seriously."

His Turn: Ellis

"I am more than willing to shoulder my portion of the blame for the demise of my marriage. When I look at old family videos, I see nothing but smiles and hear nothing but laughter. So what went wrong? So much and yet so little. I can never put Humpty-Dumpty back together, but I prefer to remember the good times, even if she doesn't."

Y Intersection: Which Road to Take?

Every troubled marriage brings the wife to a fork in the road. If he absolutely has no intention of returning home, she'll be on her own. If he says he wants to come home but his behavior indicates otherwise, she still may choose to take the single path. If both choose reconciliation, the couple will take the other route either side by side or hand in hand. If the marriage ends, the wife must protect herself and her children legally and financially. If reconciliation is planned, the couple must traverse many more miles through both alien as well as recognizable territory.

Some members, like Ginger, feel precariously balanced somewhere in between. "Ernst comes and goes, but we had a wonderful weekend watching movies, working out with our son, then he left to go somewhere else for dinner. He said not to make too many demands, then confused me by adding: 'Why do you think I come home? Because I want to!' We're both more affectionate and I don't think he's sleeping with anyone because we promised we would tell each other if that happened. For now our focus is on rebuilding our friendship. I hope I can remain strong enough to see it through."

Lee responded to Ginger. "You sound like me when I tiptoed around before James left. I figured 'this too will pass' and tried to be strong while I waited for the other shoe to drop. And drop it did. He confessed he had been deceiving me for more than a year, then left me that night!"

Inevitably, many marriages collapse under the weight of the crisis. Sometimes the wife cannot ride the endless rollercoaster; other times the man makes a unilateral decision to live without her or somewhere else. Eventually some couples who've tried to resolve their differences decide they would be better off apart.

Because Stefan maxed out their credit cards in the earliest phase of his crisis, Elinor knew finances would be an issue. After talking with her lawyer, she canceled their joint accounts and insisted on an early mediation to at least deal with assets in the interim. "I didn't want him accusing me of unfairly cutting him off, but a friend of mine had been saddled with huge debts and I couldn't afford to be in her position either."

Annie counseled one member who was afraid she would be left with nothing if she didn't take proactive steps after her husband moved in with the other woman. "Having the guts to stand up for yourself is half the battle. Now's the time to make preparations. You don't have to carry them out, but you must protect yourself. First you need to check your marital assets. Make sure you have approximately the amount of money you think you should have. Have any large sums been withdrawn from any account? If so, he may have to reimburse you for your portion in divorce proceedings. Watch for any money spent on adulterous behavior and make note of these. He does not have the right to spend any of your assets on another woman. You must put your emotional reactions on the back burner long enough to think logically. Don't worry about pushing him further away. When a man starts fiddling with the finances, the time has come to take control. We can't make them love us, but we can make them respect us!"

Lee made this list for deciding whether or not to split:

- Do I deserve this?

- Is this something I would do to someone I loved?

- Is this what I want my marriage to be like?

- How much control do I really have?

- Can I ever forgive him?

- Is life long enough to put my life on hold for an unknown amount of time?

- Is midlife crisis a good enough excuse for this behavior?

The Traveler Returns

Club members often report the first signs that their family emergency has passed with trepidation since they find it difficult to diagnose whether this is a cure or a remission.

"I'm scared this is another phase, but Martin does seem to have come out of his fog! For the past few weeks he's been affectionate, considerate, told me twice I looked lovely, and hugged me for no reason," reported Francine. "He's been so isolated and unresponsive I hardly know how to respond to this charming person. This weekend we were snowed in and had a wonderful time playing cards, watching TV, and making love for the first time in months. Afterward we both said 'I love you' and meant it. I know this could be temporary, but I hope it is not."

While the men may be anxious to win their wives' confidence, the wives who have been burnt may be reluctant to get close to the fire again. Polly spoke of her struggle to rebuild her faith in Fred. "He had to know I could not accept another infidelity. However, I was willing to pardon what happened with the other woman because it meant something had not been working in our relationship—nothing more, nothing less."

Michelle wanted to believe in Ted. She had hoped he'd apologize for hurting her, but he did not. "That was one strike against him, but I chalked it up to the end of the affair as well as withdrawal from the other woman. I looked for reassurance that he was in for the long haul. When I didn't feel as though he was trying to make up to me for what he did, that was strike two. Finally the other woman moved back to our area and I watched carefully to see what would happen. Sure enough, the affair started up again, although Ted denied it. Strike three and he was out."

Dottie's faith in Lance had been obliterated. He rebuilt it little by little by his actions. "I made a list of things that I did trust, such as his care of the kids and cars, and his work ethic. By focusing on the positive, I felt better too." Dottie made this list for how she began to heal:

- I decided I was responsible for my own actions and not his.

- I realized I could not control him.

- I agreed to take his word that it was over.

- I told him I would leave if he lied to me again.

- I accepted that I was grieving and it would hurt for a long time.

- I kept our families and our kids out of it—including not talking about his affair to anyone.

- I wrote a list of what I appreciated about him and added to it as he changed.

- I listened to how he had been and how he was now feeling.

- I didn't criticize his feelings, but accepted them as part of him.

- I decided jealousy hurt me the most and that I could overcome those emotions.

- I kept my antenna up, but didn't hunt for dirt.

- I looked for joy and ways to promote it: planting flowers in the garden, seeing a favorite movie, watching the children playing, listening to music.

- I saved good feelings when they came and tried to hang onto those moments in order to blot out the bad ones.

Just because the man may have made the decision to return, living with him may not be easy. If he had to disengage from the other woman, he may still think about her and the complications he caused in her life. He can't share his concerns or guilt with his wife and may internalize his confusion, which may create mood swings. He may continue to resent his responsibilities and may not be over the desire to flee. He has lost the dream of freedom and a less stressful life. His home represents irrevocable ties and problems. Compliments and thanks will go a long way to make him feel appreciated.

Alternate Routes: Is Divorce the Better Option?

Only each person can decide when to throw in the towel. Many go to extraordinary lengths to preserve their marriages, especially once they are over their initial shock and learn that midlife crisis may be more of a transition than a final destination. Many wonder, will he grow out of it? And if so, how long will it take? Even those who reconciled warn newcomers that the process will take far longer—and be more painful—than they can imagine.

His Turn: Harrison

"Just as someone doesn't wake up one morning with a midlife crisis, someone doesn't wake up one morning cured. For me it's been a process of questioning where I was heading, who was going with me, who I was, and how I related to everyone in my life.

"Along the way I had to find the tools to understand what was happening. We may not be able to stop how we feel, but we can learn what is happening and control our actions. If someone doesn't choose to figure this out, it may take them longer to recover or they may never get off the treadmill."

Unfortunately, a high percentage of Midlife Wives Club members were unable to salvage their marriages. "I tried and found I could not do it alone," Jan posted with some bitterness. "The self-help books were fine for me, but he wouldn't read them. I love Graham, but he's a selfish brat. I've become ill over this so I am ending it to preserve what little sanity and health I have left. I wanted to keep my family intact but Graham needs to find himself and to hell with us."

Blanche was patient for nine months, then capitulated to her husband's desire for a divorce. "Even as I signed the preliminary divorce papers—because that is what Shep wanted—I didn't give up hope that he'd snap out of it. My family congratulated me for dumping 'the jerk,' but I was miserable. They told me it was time to get on with my life, but my life was with him. So I finally stopped listening to him and the Greek chorus telling me what to do, called the attorney, and stopped the divorce from going through. Then I told Shep, 'I don't care if it takes 15 years for my best friend to come home, I'm not changing the locks.' "

"I was willing to wait," said Pat. "But when Frank went to the attorney, I knew he'd made up his mind. I had one last choice to make and I chose to let our marriage end quickly."

Francine reflected on the end of her difficult year with Martin's midlife crisis by saying, "We start out with ourselves and end up with only ourselves in the end. In between we are offered an opportunity to get to know and experience people in several areas of our lives. Each person we meet, whether good or bad, leaves an imprint on our character, but ultimately we only have ourselves."

"What I've learned is that nothing is 100 percent anyone's fault," Annie stated. "Sometimes we blame the other person for his choices; other times we berate ourselves for pushing them away. Those who make decisions that hurt us must be accountable. Yet many of us emerge from that fiery furnace to find our marriages have coalesced into something even more honest and solid. But nobody is ever the same. You will never again see your husband through the same innocent eyes. A certain degree of integrity can never be reclaimed. In order to look past these scars, each person will have to grow beyond where they started. You cannot idly wait for your husband to snap out of it. You must set the boundaries on what kind of treatment you will or won't accept and then make decisions based on what is best for you. Simply waiting for him while he lives with another woman demonstrates a lack of caring toward you. You can let him know some love remains but that you will not be mistreated. Then, if you reconcile, you can build on the foundation of self-respect that you were able to secure for yourself. And if he has been able to respect your limits during the crisis, he has proven he can be trusted in small ways. Either way, it's a winning hand."

Researcher Robert C. Peck characterized middle age as the beginning of the second half of life during which four major psychological tasks have to be mastered by men as well as by women. First, they must believe that by using their brain over brawn, they can accomplish more than they could when they were young. Next, as men and women age, they see value in each other as companions and individuals rather than as sex objects. Third, as parents die, children leave home, and work responsibilities change, spouses have to be flexible enough to shift to new ties in the community as well as the professional world and transfer emotional investments from one person to another and from one activity to another. Finally, midlife partners must master control over their own lives instead of being manipulated by external events and experiences. Some learn to use their experiences to achieve perspective and to solve new issues, while others grow increasingly rigid and block the flow of new ideas. It can take time, patience, and sometimes require professional help, yet if both husbands and wives have the will to work at it, they can make progress on these tasks as individuals and together as a couple. Together they can enter the second half of their lives with the knowledge that they have negotiated an obstacle course, mastered a crucial series of steps, and are actually stronger and more secure than they were before.

CHAPTER 10

New Vistas: Marital Outcomes—and Beyond

We pardon to the extent that we love.

—Francois, Duc de La Rochefoucauld, written in 1665, age 52

A group of Midlife Wives Club members have logged onto the website for several years, first in the throes of their emergent crises, at various times as their situations evolved, later as advisors to the new, more fragile members. They have shared their intimate stories and wisdom so that others could learn from their decisions, mistakes, and outcomes. A core group offered assistance for this book both privately and in a special section of the website. The current resolutions for some of these leading contributors whose names were followed by an asterisk (*) when they first appeared in the book are featured in this chapter. Since most members of the club join at the peak of their pain, it is helpful to learn how others survived the early stages of shock and fear and consider themselves successes, even though their stories have very different endings—or new beginnings.

Home on the Range: Reconciliation

While reconciliation concludes many of the marital rifts, club members recount it is easier when neither spouse has had an affair. Healing is usually impossible unless the relationship with the third person is irrevocably over. Even so, there is often a long period of recrimination and recuperation. Some experts suggest that it may take at least a full year to mend the fences, although the first weeks and months are the most agonizing as emotions of shame and guilt clash with blaming and bitterness. The erring spouse may feel he can never live it down—so why keep trying; the injured spouse may be unable to repress her irritation in large and small ways. This cycle may further polarize the couple, even when they have the best of intentions to try again. According to Dr. Steve and Cathy Brody, "Studies show that men are more threatened by the sexual aspects of a wife's affair, while women worry more about the degree of emotional intimacy experienced by a husband with his lover." There is some crossover of course. According to the Brodys, healing is not only hard for the spouse who has been wronged, it is also hard and surprisingly intense for the one who had the affair. They suggest honest answers to questions and expressing sincere remorse. The spouse who was hurt requires frequent reassurance that she is loved and her husband is committed to being with her. Sometimes the injured person's carping and whining may set off another fight-or-flight response. The man must remind himself of the roots of her insecurity and dig in for the long haul.

Evie worried that their marriage would never recover. "Through the darkest of days I protected our children and believed in the commitment I had made to our family. I feel like I trained for, ran, and won a marathon that I never expected to enter. The result: I like this new person better. She's more independent, honest—at least to herself—as well as more empathetic with others. I took Robert back as an equal instead of grasping at him out of an overwhelming need." Evie admitted that fears and doubts still threaten to overwhelm her. "But as long as we talk about them, we can get over them," Evie said during a hopeful time. "I know that I have grown personally and while I'm far from perfect, I have much to contribute to our partnership."

Evie and Robert
Outcome: Reconciliation

During a serious illness, steroids helped push Robert into a depression. Although Evie knew he was abnormally withdrawn, he rebuked her suggestions to seek counseling. When he couldn't sleep, he started surfing the Internet and soon this interest became an obsession. Then he insisted on a trip alone, something he had never done before. When Robert returned, he moved in with the other woman, whom he had met online. Six weeks later when she left, Robert plunged into despair. "I held his hand as a friend and directed him toward help. After crying in my arms about being dumped by the other woman, he hugged me and said, 'I just thought of something! When I left you, there was no one to comfort you.'"

Finally Robert saw a therapist. "Antidepressant medication helped him to see everything in a clearer, more realistic light." Soon they were in counseling together. "While I am not accountable for his choices," Evie said, "I acknowledge that depression made his reactions to the midlife passage more extreme. He takes responsibility for his poor decisions, accepts that depression confused his judgment, and is working with me toward a mutual future."

Just as a teenager who has blown his trust by breaking a family rule must earn back privileges, so must the errant spouse. The Brodys recommend the man calling when he is going to be late—even by a few minutes—because his partner needs reassurance that he is not with someone else. The hurt spouse may feel compelled to lash out with vindictive comments or bring up the sore subject at inappropriate times, so she must restrain the urge to retaliate. Just as a man blamed his wife for his problems as a way of projecting his negative feelings about himself, a woman may continue to blame the man as a way of projecting her anxieties.

Colleen said she couldn't make herself 20 years younger or more docile or more exciting because it was forbidden, but added, "If reconciliation is ever going to succeed, I am willing to work at anything that is within my power, even if it means giving up as much of my residual anger as possible."

Colleen and Rory
Outcome: Multiple Reconcilations

Colleen's husband found the lure of a young female student too tempting to ignore. When Colleen discovered the affair, she gave Rory an ultimatum: end the relationship or the marriage was over. Rory acquiesced reluctantly, then he engaged in several other quick liaisons. Each time, when caught, he promised it would be the last. When Colleen made plans to move to another country, Rory begged for one more chance. "He has assured me of his intention to be faithful to me in the future. I have agreed to put these, too, behind us."

Annie believes that separation helps each person understand themselves better. "Only by setting standards for ourselves as individuals—not just as Joe's wife or Mary's husband—can we contribute to that relationship in any meaningful way. I wouldn't have given you a penny's worth of hope that my marriage would have survived this crisis, but maybe a troubled relationship must come to a flash point in order to exorcise the demons within it."

Annie and Larry
Outcome: Reconciliation

When Annie discovered that Larry had been cheating, she went into a rage and threw him out of the house. She wouldn't answer his calls, changed the locks, began smoking and drinking too much, couldn't sleep soundly, and became irritated with everyone who expressed concern. Even when she learned the affair had ended long before she found out, she was so propelled by a need for revenge that she filed for divorce. Then she went online and found the Midlife Wives Club. As she conversed with the other members, she had a chance to validate her angry feelings. This led to a reexamination of her needs with more logic and less emotion. Annie reestablished communication with Larry, and they slowly shared their deepest hurts and fears.

After three years, Annie halted divorce proceedings and her husband returned home. "Please don't think this is a fairy-tale ending. I wish I could put the past in a box and bury it—as some others have been able to do—but so far that has not happened yet. Some days I don't think about it at all, yet there are others when I am obsessed by it, even if it did happen years ago. I realize this is a part of who I am, and I will have to deal with that in my own way."

The Long and Winding Road: Divorce

A large portion of the midlife marriages end in long-term separation or divorce. Club members struggle months and even years later with loneliness and fears.

Brooke wrote, "Ed left a few months ago, but I still reach for him across the bed and when I realize he's gone, I start trembling uncontrollably." After club members encouraged her to see a doctor, she reported that her shakes were diagnosed as panic attacks and medication helped. Even so, Brooke said that every time she felt armored against Ed's next assault, he would lunge from another direction. "He was so caught up with the other woman he was blind to everyone else. Finally I decided that I would make the rules about visits and calls to me as long as he was living with the other woman. The limits not only are helping me retain a smidgen of sanity, it might save our marriage if he decides she isn't worth losing what he has."

Grace gave a pep talk to several frightened new members. "Remember Gulliver was tied down by strands of fear—whether real or imagined—which drained his courage. To zap those strands, recognize that divorce can be the beginning of a better life. I made a list of my worst fears by asking these questions: What if . . .

- I live the rest of my life alone?

- I never have sex again?

- I don't have enough money?

- I have no one to share the lows and highs with on an intimate level?

- I mess up?

- I am not as confident as I think I should be?

- I don't have anything to give anyone?

To many of these I could respond 'so what?' Others made me quake, but I muddled through the way I had during the whole mess."

Flo wanted everyone to know that although she felt she had lived a nightmare for three years, it did get better. "Rodney divorced me after 30 years of marriage. Now he is having a baby with a woman our daughter's age who he met on the Internet. The stone in my heart hasn't left entirely, but I no longer notice it with every beat. The times of turmoil brought me a strength I never expected." While Flo prayed that Rodney would wake up and come back to her, he did not. Flo told club members she was able to endure by thinking only of the present. "I'd ask myself: 'Am I okay right this minute?' I avoided dwelling about the past or the future. The past is over and nobody knows the future."

Coming to grips with the legal or emotional end of a marriage is part of the grieving process. After Tish signed the finalization documents, she went home and pored over the memorabilia of her marriage from the love notes to the wedding cards to the counseling pamphlets and burned them in the fireplace. "Then I read portions of my journals from before we were married. The obvious problems leapt off the page. If I knew then what I know now! Still they helped me reflect on the pleasant part of the more innocent times."

Lee was taking stock of how far she had come and posted her list of accomplishments:

- I'm a stronger, more independent person.

- I have self-confidence I never had before.

- I went back to school and finished a degree.

- I got a job that I love, and a promotion in less than a year.

- I traveled to other cities to meet online friends.

- I'm wiser to what's really important in life.

- I don't sweat the small stuff—and most of it *is* small stuff.

- I've grown closer to my son.

- I appreciate my mother more than ever before.

- I've made a new best friend, a male, who is not a lover but understands me.

- I've fallen head over heels in love again.

- I have a stronger belief in God, and have found the perfect church.

- I'm at peace with my past. I have no regrets.

- I can be happy with or without a man.

- I don't have to change myself to be loved.

- I will continue to love James at some level forever.

Lee and James
Outcome: Divorce, New Man in Her Life

Lee was still working through her own depression after her father's death when James' father died suddenly and he became the reluctant caretaker for his obstinate mother. Shortly after his mother became a houseguest, James started an affair with a co-worker. "He said he needed to talk to someone who had suffered a similar loss—forgetting that I had been through it too." Nine months later James left, and that night Lee found the club.

Members counseled her as she dealt with divorce, parenting issues, her ex-husband's attempts to return, and her move to a different city away from negative family influences.

Just as Lee was feeling independent, a special person walked into her life. "I was shocked to learn that my heart had mended enough to open again, but it did and I am in love with a wonderful person. I don't know if it will last forever, but I'm taking the chance."

Jenelle said, "I read that divorce is a transformative experience, but didn't realize how painful it was to take a lump of clay, mold it, glaze it, then put it through the kiln of experience before it emerges an object that everyone admires. A few years ago I had no money, no job, no car, no roof over my head. My family was thousands of miles away. I had hit bottom, but knew the only way to survive was to better myself. I finished a master's degree, found a better job, and soon was self-supporting. Learning to laugh again was another turning point. Three years after my divorce, I found a caring man and we are still together. Sometimes tragedies are gifts in disguise."

Carl Jung, the psychiatrist who defined many of the seminal midlife issues, wrote, "Everything that irritates us about others can lead us to an understanding of ourselves." Many club members look back on the journey grateful that they were forced to reexamine their lives. Others are haunted by thoughts of "the way it used to be" and wish they could recapture the former bliss or an elusive fantasy that never existed.

"I hate to say this," Tish admitted, "but I never should have married Marv. Do I have regrets? Yes, for the misery everyone went through, but also no, because I had to make those mistakes to get to this point."

Emily had rushes of buoyant feelings every time Gabe was

kind to her. "Eighteen months after the divorce, when Gabe made a physical advance, I was flattered and hopeful. The next time I saw him, he was his typical surly self." Emily's tug-of-war with Gabe was a difficult pattern to break. "I was used to the feel of the rope sliding back and forth between my fingers. When I had him coming toward me, I felt great, but it was short-lived. Eventually, I had to let go. My final regret was that the other woman would reap the benefit of what we had learned together." But now that it is over, Emily said she is sometimes tempted to send Gabe a thank-you note. "From the moment he walked out the door, my better life began—even though I didn't know it at the time. My need to learn more about midlife crisis got me reading voraciously. That led to other explorations."

Emily and Gabe
Outcome: Divorce

Emily and Gabe faced myriad midlife conflicts. They disagreed on discipline for their teenagers; he was resentful that she could run a successful business from home while he worked overtime to avoid being laid off. When she became depressed after a hysterectomy, he moved out to "find himself." Gabe attempted a brief return home, but he refused to stop seeing the other woman. He didn't want to relinquish his wife either. "Finally, I filed for divorce, not because I was tired of his shenanigans, but because I hoped it would shock him into returning." Even after the divorce was final, Emily thought there was a chance he'd return someday. In the meantime she helped the kids through their adolescent years and took college courses to prepare for a career change.

Two years after the divorce, Emily accepted that she had to move on without Gabe. "Not only is the other woman still in his life, but he has another on the side as well! I'm glad I'm out of that mess—at last."

My Way or the Highway: Picking up the Pieces

It's over. He's left, she has kicked him out, or the two of you have come to a mutual agreement. Club members find it difficult to pick up the pieces when it is irrevocably over. "Moving on is so hard," Grace admitted. "It's the death of promises and expectations. It's looking at empty drawers or closets filled with stuff that he's left behind. Do you box it up? Leave it there? There are practical considerations. Emotional ones. Where to begin?"

Like many members of the club, Kelly's first priority was to go back to school. Since many married "too young" and started families early, their own educations had been truncated. Some signed up for vocational training like cosmetology and practical nursing while others worked on unfinished degrees. "Education is wasted on the young," Kelly proclaimed. "I never loved school before, but this time I do. It also takes my mind off my problems, plus I am meeting a new social set. I recommend that everyone do something they had put on hold over the last few years."

Stan
Outcome: Divorce and Online Romance

When Stan, one of many men at the Midlife Wives Club, joined the forum at age 38, he declared himself happily married to his second wife. "I thought I was starting to go through manic depression, but the pieces didn't fit, although midlife crisis did." He also saw a familial pattern because his father traded his first wife for a younger woman—Stan's mother—during his midlife years.

Stan joined a gym, lost weight, and found himself attracted to a much younger woman even though his wife was pregnant with their first child. He fought the first temptation by reading self-help books and talking to club members, but succumbed to a second opportunity, thus ending his marriage. His wife got the lion's share of their possessions while they shared custody of their baby daughter. "Midlife crisis is a lot like bull riding. It's rough and you get stomped on, kicked, and gored from time to time, but if you can hold on until the whistle, you will be better equipped for the next rank bull."

A year after his divorce Stan told club members about the new woman in his life, a woman whose marriage had recently ended due to her own husband's midlife crisis. The best part? He'd met Tish in the Midlife Wives Club!

As much as club members hope that their husbands will snap out of it or that they will wake and find they have only been dreaming, some realize what they want most is closure. "I'd give anything if Marv could work out the details of our divorce in a fair and square way instead of all his lying and machinations," Tish said as she recounted her woes dealing with lawyers and accountants. "I wish we could have mediated a solution, but he's too self-centered. He's fuming that he has to live on half of what we had jointly, but whose fault is that?"

No matter how upbeat the woman may try to be, no matter how much progress she has made, her ex-partner's voice on the phone, an inquisitive question from a child, an old photograph of a harmonious holiday can set her back. When Harry called Gretchen to discuss a book he was reading about separations—one she had tried to get him to look at a year earlier—she became irate. "I took a bath to calm down, then slept for almost two days. I thought I was over the worst of it. Has anyone else regressed like this?"

Other club members related how hot flashes of anger would overtake them at unsuspecting times.

Reasons for anger:

- Your life changed and someone forgot to tell you it was coming.

- Your choices were none.

- Even with choices, you can still be mad.

- Anger helps you detach.

Controlling anger:

- You can choose to be angry and decide when you stop.

- Don't let the anger become a way of life.

- Don't let anger be the focal point.

- If you control the anger, you control yourself.

- If anger takes over, you have lost again.

Ways to deal with anger:

- Pound pillows, shout in the attic, break shards for potting, knead bread.

- Exercise when the anger builds. You'll work harder, burn more calories, and feel better.

- Try kick boxing, karate, and other sports that teach controlled martial arts.

- Save some for your counselor. She'll use it to help you understand yourself better.

- Don't hurt yourself by drinking, taking drugs, or over-spending.

- Don't take it out on the kids or act it out in front of them either.

Elinor said, "I sometimes have a 'relapse' where I sit on the couch and stare at mindless TV for days at a time. It feels like a mini-depression. I've resigned myself to knowing I'm going to be fighting my way uphill for a long time to come."

Emily divulged her secret coping method. "When I get into a funk, I allow myself two days to 'veg' by sleeping, lounging, reading, watching TV, eating whatever I want, crying, or moping. But when the 48 hours are up, I force myself back into the rat race. Allowing myself to *feel* the sadness helps to relieve it, but if you can't get out of bed after two days, then you need professional help."

His Turn: Harper

"Lessons for men in male midlife crisis:

1. Make sure you don't do anything that is counter to your core values. You can change without destroying your basic beliefs. In fact, now is the time you need them most.

2. Spend time thinking about what you want—besides a potential other woman. (She's a symptom for what else might be missing in your life.)

3. Make an action plan. First work on yourself, then on your communication with your wife. Even if you thought it was

okay, read one of John Gray's Mars/Venus books. You'll see why she may not be getting your hints.

4. If you have kids, give them plenty of attention and join in as many activities as possible. If your marriage flops, you will need to have an even better bond with them if they are going to survive.

5. Evaluate your health. If you have been losing weight, have had trouble sleeping or concentrating, or feel frustrated, you are probably depressed. Don't throw your life away because you were too proud to talk to your doctor. While you are there, get your prostate checked too. (It is time, old man!)

6. Monitor your consumption of alcohol, which is a depressant and will interfere with sleep. Also ration the coffee and colas and stop at noon. These may have not bothered you in the past, but your body changes.

7. Give something back to your community."

After years of living with a helpmate, some club members struggle to maintain homes alone. When a shutter is banging, the car won't start, the driveway needs shoveling, it is a double-whammy to be without the customary assistance. Some men lend a hand in emergencies, especially if children are involved, but many members log on with concerns about how they are going to take down the Christmas lights from the eaves, start the snow blower, or remove a fallen limb. Felice won the self-reliance prize with this post: "When my husband left, there were dozens of unfinished projects. On my own I've put siding on the breezeway and garage, installed gutters and downspouts, done electrical and plumbing repairs, installed carpet on the basement stairs, sealed the foundation, and much more."

Needing support after her divorce, Flo moved from the southwest to the northeast to be nearer to her daughters. "Even on days when I would rather have stayed in bed, I pushed myself to get up and go. Every time I got in the car I got lost, but I was determined to make a new life. I joined a singles group and participated in sports. My attitude is different now. I appreciate everything around me more. I reach out to people and have been rewarded with many new friends. Although it is hard to leave familiar surroundings, being with those I love most is the best decision I've ever made."

Visas to Foreign Countries: The Art of Apology

What leads most people to the Midlife Wives Club website is a search for answers. While their personal life situation may not change, they get a short course in the issues. As psychoanalyst and author Erich Fromm wrote, "Understanding a person does not mean condoning; it only means that one does not accuse him as if one were God or a judge placed above him." Nothing diffuses volatile situations better than comprehension. The wisdom of remaining friends with a man who deserted his family during separation or after divorce is a topic for debate.

Nora reported that after more than a year of being at each other's throats, she and Sven became civil. "We apologized for hurting each other in the early days when we spoke in anger. Now we go out of our way to accommodate the other and are flexible, polite, and courteous. After 24 years—18 married—we can't hate each other. There were too many good times, and being apart allows us to focus on those. If we had stayed together, I am sure we would not be treating each other this well."

Kristin recently negotiated real estate contracts to sell her marital home and purchase a new one for herself, decisions and actions she would have never have contemplated doing alone in years past. "I will never go back to the bleakness of that abyss even though I needed to visit it to arrive where I am today: stronger, healthier, and more confident in my ability to make myself happy."

For more than a month Kristin and Dan worked together to pack up their home. "At times it was stressful. There were moments we cried. After each session we went to dinner at a local tavern. The last weekend the owner came over, introduced himself, and bought us a few rounds. Dan introduced me as his wife without further explanation and said we'd be back. I guess we will. We've been sharing CDs, and although he's getting the blender, I'm borrowing it for a party. I don't know where this will lead—and I have no illusions—but it may become another level of a relationship, or perhaps a friendship. I only hope it won't come back to bite me in the butt."

Emily warned Kristin that Dan's camaraderie might be another form of manipulation. "He's gotten rid of the house, his responsibilities, and has his freedom. You are around when he wants to have dinner and share music. How convenient for him! But if you become interested in another man, Dan may show another side. Also, don't expect him to fill the role of companion. Find new ones for yourself because the moment you need him, he may not be there. Enjoy the friendly playing field, but remember it can turn into a battlefield in a few quick moves."

Megan concurred with Emily. "George and I have been able to maintain a 'friendship' since we split," Megan told the group, "but I use quotation marks because even though I'd rather it be friendly than hostile—especially for the children's sake—I have a problem equating a considerate man with one who left his family for someone else. And while he reveals little animosity toward me, he treats my fiancé with contempt."

Kristin and Dan
Outcome: Divorce, But Remain Friends

Kristin's husband was angry and depressed, but she couldn't pinpoint the reason. Eventually he moved out. They continued to date over the next year even after she caught Dan in bed with another woman. When she told him she wanted a divorce, Dan rallied for another try. As soon as a second infidelity surfaced, Kristin renewed divorce proceedings. Dealing with Dan's crisis pushed Kristin to the brink of a collapse; her physical health suffered and her family was concerned for her emotional health. When self-preservation finally took over, she started seeing a therapist, found the club, began exercising regularly, and accepted a new job. "With each step I became stronger and more resolved in my quest to put my life back together, with or without my spouse."

Kristin and Dan remain friends but she is no longer desperate to have him as an integral part of her life. "I have learned that you can't control another person's feelings; you can only learn to love yourself and give yourself the gift of happiness."

Few newcomers even understood the term "midlife crisis" before finding the website. Occasionally both husband and wife logged on to the club. Sometimes they knew each other's identity. Sometimes they didn't. Most hid their relationship from the group. (And like so many online communities, some romances flourished as well!) Cheryl and Ozzie offered the Midlife Wives Club a unique perspective on reconciliation because they each contributed points of view during his crisis.

On her twenty-first wedding anniversary, Cheryl summed up her horrible year. "One day and one year ago, Ozzie gave me 'the speech.' Now we are living in his apartment as a retreat and I have become fond of this place, which surprises me. At first it represented pain and resentment because he lived here with her. We had little contact for almost a year and thought divorce was more likely than reconciliation because we each were stuck on either side of a wide chasm. He had too much pride to apologize and I felt he could never repair the damage. I told Ozzie that I never wanted to feel that insecure again."

His Turn: Ozzie

"After 20 years of marriage, I wanted to live without being responsible to someone day and night. We married at 20 because she was pregnant, and I've felt trapped ever since. I had an affair with someone I met at work, lied about it, then left when I thought I was in love with the other woman.

"Finally, Cheryl told me she wanted closure. At that moment I was trying to find my way back to her, but didn't think she would accept me. I realized I dodged a bullet, but I'm not out of the danger zone yet. We have to work out a way to heal her hurt. My actions were awful and most women would refuse to forgive me. Cheryl's willingness to do so is grace.

"I can't expect her forgiveness, though, without taking responsibility for what I did. There were better ways for me to deal with my problems. I should have listened to the warning signals. I should have admitted I didn't know everything. I was arrogant and full of myself. I was searching in the dark for what was already in my hands. I wish I could make it go away as if it never happened, but that is impossible. All I can do is help her find peace with me. I am here because I love her. Part of loving her is to make her happy future my responsibility."

Scenic Overlook: Falling in Love Again

Tish said she could not contemplate relationships like those that Megan and Kristin described. "Even a truce would be welcome, although I doubt it will ever come." Despite her fractured relationship with her ex-husband, Tish found happiness in an unexpected way. "When all I could see were looming storm clouds, I never imagined the sun would ever shine again," Tish told club members when she admitted she had fallen in love. "Now the skies are clear and full of hope. When I was lost, I started pastoral counseling. With the Lord's help I was able to sign the divorce papers. As soon as I did, a burden was lifted from me. I'm grateful to have learned much while traversing this road."

Tish and Marv
Outcome: Divorce, Online Romance

When Tish first joined the club, she and Marv were in the midst of their legal separation and she was in counseling. Tish thought that living apart would bring Marv to his senses, but his refusal to give up the other woman ignited hostile divorce proceedings. She was determined not to lose her home and everything she'd worked for. "At least we didn't have children," Tish said.

When the legalities were over, Tish told club members, "Out of pain came renewal and love." What she didn't share publicly was that her new relationship was with Stan—one of the men in the club whose marriage had ended due to his midlife crisis.

"Is there life after midlife crisis?" Bonnie asked rhetorically. "You bet! Now I:

- Say exactly what I think or feel.

- Am closer to my daughter.

- Hang up when Nigel is being disrespectful.

- Don't have to kowtow to him ever again.

- Am stronger than I believed.

- Find I don't need a man to validate me.

- Can run a tension-free household.

- Can make a better life for myself."

Falling in love again is a minefield that some Midlife Wives Club members rush into, while others tiptoe terrified that they might step on a trigger wire. Joan became engaged rather soon after her divorce from Roy. "I'm head over heels although everyone warns me about rebound. He was also divorced around the same time. So what if I'm his rebound?"

Tish responded, "If you continue to question yourself, there is a reason for the question. When I fell in love again, I had doubts, but with each passing day, the fears fell away and the trust grew—not only about him, but myself and my judgment. Go with your gut. Let it develop, but don't rush."

His Turn: Ellis

"Am I ever going to love again? Can I ever love again? Do I want to love again? Yes! But only if I let myself heal and forgive. Trusting someone else will be the hard part. I gave my wife unconditional love and it didn't work out, but everyone else I've given to does love me, which I consider a decent return on my investment."

When Gretchen was in the final stages of divorcing Harry, she started dating again. Within a short time she had two lovers vying for her attention—a situation she found both heady and scary. "While it's exciting, I've become more sensitive to what I need. One guy didn't call or respond to my e-mails so I told him I did not need that type of rejection at this point in my life. The other fellow is a sweetheart and good company. Having two at once has advantages because I feel so wanted after feeling so abandoned, but it demands a lot of my time."

"Believe it or not, I think I've found the silver lining," Megan told the club. "When the crisis first came, I thought I was going to die. In the end George's actions set me free. I met a person who respects me the way I have always wanted to be treated. Sometimes I wish this would have happened even earlier in my life because now I feel like I wasted many years, but I know I had to traverse that obstacle course to be the person I am now."

Megan and George
Outcome: Divorce, New Man in Her Life

Megan's husband tried to buy his way out of depression when he sold his successful business, but a fancy new home, expensive toys, and fast cars didn't fill the void. When George began spending time with the other woman, their marriage started unraveling. After George gave Megan the infamous "I love you, but I'm not in love with you" speech, she asked him to leave while he decided what he wanted. Counseling didn't resolve their problems and they divorced.

When Megan met the next man in her life, she was in for a pleasant surprise: Sex was more satisfying than ever. "George had me believing I was frigid. It turns out he was a lazy, lousy lover. Before, sex was a chore; now I can't get enough!"

Passports to Freedom: Forgiveness

"Ben wants to come home, but how can I let him?" asked Barb. "He was intimate with the other woman for too long. I can't imagine being close to him again. I should have thrown him out the minute I discovered what was happening. You have to be pretty special to be able to forgive what he's done. If anyone has, please tell me your secret, because I can't!"

"I have not been able to forgive Nigel for all the destruction he caused. I can't forgive him for staying married all those years if he was unhappy," Bonnie told the club. "I can't forgive him for what he did to our daughter. I can't forgive him for the other woman—who was his boss—or destroying her marriage and children as well. I can't forgive him for the STD he gave me. I can't forgive him for saying he loved me a week prior to asking for the divorce. I can't forgive him for calling me nasty names. Maybe in time I will be able to understand everything, I'm just not there yet."

Neither are most Midlife Wives Club members, especially when adultery has been part of the scenario. "Don't you see who this is eating up?" Francine asked Barb and Bonnie. "Your anger is controlling you, not him. Yes, his actions were hurtful, thoughtless, unacceptable, mean, hateful, and cowardly, but he can't take them back. If you don't let go, it will cripple you both. You need to forgive him for *your* sake. He knows he screwed up and he will carry that burden forever. If you can forgive him, maybe he can move on to forgive himself. I'll bet he would be the most grateful creature on earth. It's cruel to hold someone in bondage. It's a gift to release someone from it. So forgive and forget, like God does for all our stupid mistakes. I left it between him and God and I bowed out."

Megan believed that forgiveness requires remorse on the part of the guilty party. She said that until she heard a heartfelt apology, forgiveness was not an option. "I'm not bitter. I will forgive George the day he acknowledges the pain he put his family through. Until then—no way!"

Norman Cousins wrote, "The tragedy of life is not death, but what we let die inside of us while we live." This might be applied to our capacity for forgiveness, which does not seem to come naturally. How do we get to a place where we can pardon? Is any one person entirely to blame? Aren't there two people in every marriage, in every fight? While many Midlife Wives Club members felt blindsided by the crisis and subsequent avalanche, they must have contributed to some of the snow drifts that built up on the slope. Everyone makes mistakes. Everyone has unintentionally hurt someone they loved. There are sins of commission as well as omission: hugs they didn't give, kisses they didn't offer freely, times they were too self-involved, words they shouldn't have said, moods they should have kept to themselves, money they shouldn't have spent. In the equation of marriage, a wife's small wrongs may not balance his big one—at least in her mind—but they combined with other life forces (his childhood, his health, his genetics, his profession) to propel him into the calamity.

Colleen explained that once she decided to take Rory back, forgiveness was part of her mindset. "In some of my reading about rebuilding marriages, it said that before forgiveness can work, the hurt spouse must be adequately compensated by the offending party. However, the injured party also must realize that the perpetrator had some unmet needs that led to the affair and should try and meet some of his conditions. The point is that something was missing for each spouse. Even so, I have trouble accepting that anything was my fault."

"If I walked up to Sid and said, 'I forgive you,' he'd reply, 'For what?' I am tired of finding fault, tired of blaming, replaying events, and wondering if I did this or that, maybe he'd still be here," Savannah posted. "So I let go and forgave. I went through what I needed to in order to grow: the sadness, frustration, loneliness, depression, the anger. Finally I told myself not to waste any more emotions. Sid didn't intend to hurt me—he was just ill-equipped to deal with his midlife issues. I don't regret anything because from the ashes has risen the Phoenix."

"If I forgive Zach, does that mean it was all right?" Josie asked. "What would it change for me? How can I forget an episode that left me confused about what love really means? I never got an explanation, let alone an apology."

"Is acceptance the same as forgiveness?" Nora wondered. "Even if I can accept what Sven did to me, I can't forgive how he hurt our sons."

While forgiveness is a common theme in religion, the emotional benefits of forgiveness are receiving renewed attention in the mental health field. In his book *The Forgiving Self: The Road from Resentment to Connection*, clinical psychologist Dr. Robert Karen says that forgiving someone because you think you "should" is worse than not forgiving them at all because forgiveness "entails an important, internal process" that should not be rushed. One element of sincere forgiveness is when the parties involved learn to express their anger appropriately, to learn to "enjoy their anger" without holding a grudge or exploding. Karen points out that when two people are in conflict, "who needs to forgive and who needs to apologize is often a toss-up. In most situations, everyone shares some blame." Those who refuse to forgive injure themselves since they must endure the gnawing resentment.

In order to cope, people often hold someone else accountable for their misery. Just as club members complain about being blamed during their man's crisis, they in turn berate their spouses for their disloyalty. While the spurned person may rationalize her stance, *she* continues to carry the weight of pain, and *she* does not heal. Karen speaks of blame as being "absorbent, soaking up sadness, and providing a target for fury." He points out that ultimately, to forgive is to let go of our pride, our fear, and our resentment and make peace with our losses. For most club members this means the loss of a sacred trust, of a valued friendship, or the future a couple planned. In the end, the person who wields the power is the one who forgives, not the one holding the grudge.

"Forgiveness is the ability to stop using what he did 'wrong' as the yardstick to measure his future actions, but I'm not entirely there yet," Evie confessed. "While wounds heal eventually, some scars never do. So with time I hope to forgive, but I can't imagine forgetting."

According to the Dalai Lama, the most important step in forgiveness is to recognize the wrongfulness of the act and to learn from it. When asked if it is better to just forget about the act, he replied, "If you forget about it, then forgiveness would have no meaning. Underlying forgiveness is the ability to distinguish between the individual and the act." The Dalai Lama reminds us that at various times in our lives everyone needs someone to forgive them for something and someone to show them compassion, and thus we should treat other people with respect, even if we feel they've wronged us.

"It took two people to end our marriage," Emily added. "Neither of us will forget the hurt we inflicted or endured, but I feel compassion for Gabe and his problems and that helps me forgive him. Besides, only a few people will leave a life-long imprint the way Gabe did. Most of it was positive, and I elected to discard what wasn't and remember what was."

Even as Midlife Wives Club members debate forgiveness, most divulge they have been unable to rid themselves of all vestiges of rage. Some believe it will take years to heal; others don't think they will ever resolve their anger. While exoneration may not come naturally, those who have been able to reach that level realize that forgiveness is a gift they give themselves.

Jasmine admitted that she couldn't help feeling angry at Rudy even when she willed herself to let go. "I had an inner voice reminding me of every lousy thing he did. I could remember the nastiest remarks from the lowest times but could hardly recall the loving moments in the years before that."

Elinor agreed that her lack of compassion was hurting both her and Stefan. "It played havoc with my physical and emotional health and helped prolong my depression. I couldn't get beyond what he had done, even though he begged for forgiveness. It was like we were in opposite jail cells and neither of us had the key." Elinor's therapist explained that she had drawn an emotional line just short of forgiveness. "When I argued that I didn't want to give in to another one of his demands and that he didn't deserve to be free of guilt, she asked, 'Do you want to heal your marriage?' Of course I did. 'Then why deny yourself the most important tool?' She said it was as though we had a joint bank account and he took 90 percent of it without my permission. Unfortunately, he invested it unwisely and now he had to build it again. She asked how long I expected Stefan to repay this eternal debt? Couldn't love cancel it and couldn't we start fresh, each enriching our bank account with new deposits of love and consideration? Although I didn't understand it at the time, eventually I saw that letting go of resentment gave me freedom and brought me more love and happiness into my life. When I was ready to let go, I became less critical and smiled more, and our love life improved. I felt whole for the first time in years. I'm not saying it was easy. Forgiving was a difficult choice, but the person most hurt by holding a grudge is the one who is upset all the time—and that was me."

"That sounds noble," Delia answered, "but how can I ever forget what Colin did to me?"

"Forgiveness is not the same as forgetting," Elinor answered. "I'll always remember, but as soon as I made up my mind to help bring that bank account up to where it had been by adding as much as I could, the intense emotions faded. In the beginning forgiveness was a calculated decision to start with a clean slate. It was difficult, but the eternal tension was worse."

Dr. Jeanne Safer, the author of *Forgiving & Not Forgiving: Why It's Sometimes Better Not to Forgive*, suggests that under some circumstances forgiving is not possible. She calls her approach "mature unforgiveness" and believes it is possible to conquer bitterness without actually forgiving. She agrees—as do many club members—that there are some situations in which someone cannot be true to herself unless she holds the perpetrator accountable. Safer also says that forgiveness is a process like grief and mourning that cannot be rushed. She suggests that someone can forgive without having to forget the action or love the person, even if it was someone like a parent, child, or spouse who betrayed them. Feeling neutral—without hate—is also a form of freedom.

"Sometimes we have to consciously choose to forgive," Annie said. "And for those who move on, forgiving can be life-changing. It may take more to forgive a failed relationship than it does to forgive a reconciled one because the person must find ways to pardon a multitude of hurts and sins without the help of the other partner."

Jenelle explained that recovery sometimes takes one step forward, two steps back. "Some days I am resolute; others I am unsure. Forgiveness is tough and maybe it depends on how valuable the relationship is. I admit I wanted my husband to act contrite and kiss my you-know-what for a long time, but scolding him made me feel lonelier. It was better for all of us to make up, make peace, make love. There was a ripple effect that helped the children too."

"Keith arranged for us both to get counseling, but I refused to forgive," Vivian admitted ruefully. "My therapist told me that if I couldn't let go, my resentment would spill over and hurt others. As long as I was punishing Keith, I was punishing myself more. Now I want to see what happens if I place faith in God and my marriage."

"I've learned that happiness is a decision. Forgiveness is a decision. Both choices have made me a better person," Vanda said.

What a Long, Strange Trip It's Been

Whether the marriage ultimately survives or splinters; whether the spouses are friends or foes; whether the wife remains in her old home, moves to a new dwelling, or a thousand miles away, the journey metaphor is the one most commonly summoned to describe club members' life-altering transitions. Lee said, "They call this a crisis, but I renamed it a journey, one I don't want to end because I don't ever again want to feel so secure that life can shake me up and spit me out. All we have is today, and tomorrow is what dreams are made of." After James left, Lee said she was like a kid tossed into a pond and forced to swim, but the predicament taught her coping skills. "I can't look to the future anymore because I have no clue where it will take me. As of this minute, this hour, this day, I'm content. Everything has been infinitely better since I took the wheel. Life is opening an unknown door for me, and I'm about to step through it with more self-assurance than ever before."

His Turn: Harrison

"I keep hearing about one door closing and another opening, but to me, life is not a row of doors, but rather a vast panorama of possibilities. Each decision reveals multiple and intersecting worlds including some doors that you thought were sealed. Maybe I've been reading too much quantum physics, but the point is that life is not linear. There is no single cause and effect. Enjoy all the choices, variations, permutations, and surprises!"

"I used to wonder whether the waiting was wasted. Now I see it was a time to store strength like a daffodil bulb," Annie offered. "Without winter dormancy, the daffodil won't burst into flower in spring. There are no shortcuts. I looked for all of them, but failed to find any. To everything there is a season. One way or another the next one will come."

Emily concluded, "Who knows what the future will bring? I may spend the rest of my life alone and if I do, that's okay. I've proven that I can support myself and that I'm a good mother. If another man comes along, I'll be a far better wife because I'm a better person than I was before. Today I laugh, I sing, I sit on my deck in the woods and watch the sunset and think, life is good!"

"As painful as the separation process was," said Pat, "I'm grateful for having gone through it. I learned new survival skills, refocused my life in a rewarding direction, and have had experiences that would never have been possible if Frank and I had remained together. We shared a 'moment in time' and it was great while it lasted but now both of us have been able to move on to lives that better suit the people we have become."

Alma summed her story up a year after her crisis began. "I look back at the hell that I went through emotionally and I see now that it was something I had to do. I will never be the person I was, but this journey has changed me and I like the new me. I've been able to rise above his midlife crisis and create a rainbow after the storm. Thanks for pulling me through a very dark time, for helping me to look inside myself, for offering me insight into what Nelson was going through, and for giving me an anonymous place to just hurt and be me."

Like Alma, members often give updates and credit the information and friendship offered by the club with helping them through one of the most difficult periods of their life. This book distills much of that wisdom, but for those who need ongoing support, don't forget to check in online.

"At moments I lost my will to live," Josie said. "Zach and I were not going in the right direction—at least not one I wanted. I was becoming someone I didn't want to be and disintegrated further trying to keep him. Grieving offered a lucidity that changed my focus to what is most important and I put trivial, material pursuits aside. Finally I am on course again and following my true compass. My intuition has intensified. I have become more open and understanding toward others. In hindsight I realize I was more lost before he decided to leave me than I am now on my own. I no longer have the nagging feeling that something is missing. I have an inner peace I never thought possible. As we talked about what mattered, I became closer to old friends. And I made some new ones in 'real' life and here at the Midlife Wives Club. Thanks for sharing the tough times, thanks for everything you taught me, your wisdom, your humor. You've changed my life."

Guidebooks and Road Maps

And the end of all our exploring
Will be to arrive where we started
And know the place for the first time.

—T. S. Eliot, written in 1935, age 57

Websites

An Internet search for "male midlife crisis" retrieves a long list of pages and websites. These selected sites provide information on midlife crisis as well as other pertinent issues including adultery, depression, and divorce. The authors do not endorse these websites nor do they take responsibility for the content or accuracy of any information they contain. The authors also do not recommend or endorse any specific organization, product, or service, nor can they guarantee that the content currently included in the sites is the same as when the site was reviewed for inclusion in this listing. The Midlife Wives Club keeps an up-to-date resource page with direct links to many of these websites.

The Midlife Wives Club (*www.midlifewivesclub.com*) was originated by Pat Gaudette, and is the website that not only inspired but provided material for this book. It offers her groundbreaking essay "His Midlife Crisis!" as well as an interactive forum for men and women dealing with their—or their partner's—midlife crisis. Members are located throughout the world and usually someone can be found either posting to the forum or in one of the chat rooms any time of the day or night.

- To log on, visit www.midlifewivesclub.com

- You can either read Pat Gaudette's introductory essay "His Midlife Crisis: Will Your Relationship Survive?", or click on the link for the Midlife Forum.

- Once you register, you can read or post to the forum, check out the Thread for Newcomers, and use the many other features.

Middle Age (*www.middleage.org*) was started in 1998 by Bob Adams as a personal website for his essays about midlife and insights into his own midlife passage.

Midlife Dimensions (*www.midlife.com*) is Jim Conway's site selling books and tapes and offering articles on midlife crises, depression, and affairs from a Christian perspective.

Midlife Passages (*www.midlife-passages.com*) was established by Andrew and Caroline Dott. He is an obstetrician-gynecologist; she is a psychotherapist. It focuses on aspects of male and female midlife.

Our Best Years (*www.bestyears.com*) was established by columnist Dr. Mike Bellah and features his midlife essays, a book list, and archived pages from his previous forum.

Halftime (*www.halftime.org*) is Bob Buford's site to help business and professional men successfully transition through midlife. It includes articles and resources for books and tapes.

Suddenly Senior (*www.suddenlysenior.com*) is Frank Kaiser's fun place for people over 50. Kaiser reinvented himself after 50 when he began writing a syndicated column describing his life as a "geezer."

Power Surge (*www.power-surge.com*) was created by Alice Lotto Stamm to address the issues of women at menopause and beyond. It includes chat rooms, message boards, articles, and lists of books and resources.

Dear Peggy (*www.dearpeggy.com*) was founded by Peggy and James

Vaughan, a husband-wife consulting team whose marriage has survived despite Jim's affairs. They have written books, conducted seminars, and founded the Center for Life-Design aimed at helping people improve the quality of their lives. Their site features articles, resource lists, and links to local support groups for people, married or divorced, who are dealing with the emotional impact of a partner's affair.

Surviving Infidelity (*www.survivinginfidelity.com*) is a site for those who have been affected by infidelity. It provides an interactive forum and articles written mainly by visitors to the site.

Divorce Support (*www.divorcesupport.about.com*) is Pat Gaudette's divorce support site offering articles, links, a chat room, and several active forums.

Divorce Busting (*www.divorcebusting.com*) is author Michele Weiner-Davis' site, which features articles, resources, an active forum, and a listing of "Keeping Love Alive" groups throughout the United States.

You Married Him (*www.youmarriedhim.com*) is designed for women and is focused on marriage and relationships. It is a large site with games, forums, advice, contests, and newsletters.

Awakenings (*www.lessons4living.com*) is the creation of clinical psychologist Dan Johnston. The site, in addition to some excellent midlife essays, contains essays, books, and a newsletter on depression, stress, and other life experiences.

Recommended Reading

The following books have been recommended by various members of the Midlife Wives Club. As with the websites listed above, they deal with many of the issues confronting couples caught in the midst of midlife crisis.

Anderson, Susan. *The Journey from Abandonment to Healing.* Berkley Publishing Group, 2000.

Bilicki, Bettie Youngs and Masa Goetz. *Getting Back Together: How to Create a New Loving Relationship with Your Old Partner and Make It Last.* Adams Media Corporation, 1995.

Brehony, Kathleen A. *Awakening in Midlife: A Guide to Reviving Your Spirits, Recreating Your Life, and Returning to Your Truest Self*. Riverhead Books, 1997.

Browne, Marlene M. *The Divorce Process: Empowerment through Knowledge*. 1st Books Library, 2001.

Conway, Jim. *Men in Midlife Crisis*. Chariot Victor, 1997.

Conway, Jim and Sally. *Moving On after He Moves Out*. Intervarsity Press, 1995.

———. *When a Mate Wants Out*. Zondervan Publishing House, 1992.

Dalai Lama, His Holiness and Howard C. Cutler, M.D. *The Art of Happiness: A Handbook for Living*. Riverhead Books, 1998.

Diamond, Jed. *Surviving Male Menopause: A Guide for Women and Men*. Sourcebooks, 2000.

———. *You Can't Say That to Me: Stopping the Pain of Verbal Abuse—An 8 Step Program*. John Wiley & Sons, 1995.

Elgin, Suzette Haden. *The Gentle Art of Verbal Self-Defense*. Prentice Hall, 2000.

Evans, Patricia. *Verbal Abuse Survivors Speak Out: On Relationship and Recovery*. Adams Media Corporation, 1993.

Gray, John. *Mars and Venus Together Forever: A Practical Guide to Creating Lasting Intimacy*. Harper Mass Market Paperbacks, 1998.

———. *Men Are from Mars, Women Are from Venus: A Practical Guide for Improving Communication and Getting What You Want in Your Relationships*. HarperCollins, 1992.

Gullo, Steven, Ph.D. and Connie Church. *Loveshock: How to Recover from a Broken Heart and Love Again*. Simon and Schuster, 1988.

Jones, Ann and Susan Schechter. *When Love Goes Wrong: What to Do when You Can't Do Anything Right*. Harper Perennial, 1993.

Marta, Suzy Yehl. *Healing the Hurt, Restoring the Hope: How to Guide Children and Teens through Times of Divorce, Death, and Crisis with the Rainbows Approach*. Rodale, 2003.

McGraw, Phillip C., Ph.D. *Relationship Rescue: A Seven-Step Strategy for Reconnecting with Your Partner*. Hyperion, 2000.

————. *Self Matters: Creating Your Life from the Inside Out*. Simon & Schuster, 2001.

Norwood, Robin. *Women Who Love Too Much: When You Keep Wishing and Hoping He'll Change*. Pocket Books, 1991.

Oxenhandler, Noelle and Nancy Hilliard. *A Grief out of Season: When Your Parents Divorce in Your Adult Years*. Little, Brown & Company, 1991.

Raffel, Lee and Jean Houston. *Should I Stay or Go: How Controlled Separation Can Save Your Marriage*. McGraw-Hill, 1995.

Real, Terrence. *I Don't Want to Talk about It: Overcoming the Secret Legacy of Male Depression*. Fireside, 1998.

Rich, Phil and Lita L. Schwartz. *The Healing Journey through Divorce: Your Journal of Understanding and Renewal*. John Wiley & Sons, 1999.

Robinson, John C. *Death of a Hero, Birth of the Soul: Answering the Call of Midlife*. Council Oak Distribution, 1997.

Rodriguez, Stephanie. *Time to Stop Pretending*. Paul S. Eriksson, 1999.

Sadler, William A., Ph.D. *The Third Age: Six Principles of Growth and Renewal after Forty*. Perseus Books, 1999.

Sanna, Lucy. *How to Romance the Man You Love—The Way He Wants You To*. Gramercy, 1999.

Schnarch, David. *Passionate Marriage: Love, Sex, and Intimacy in Emotionally Committed Relationships*. Henry Holt, 1998.

Sheehy, Gail. *New Passages: Mapping Your Life across Time*. Random House, 1995.

————. *Understanding Men's Passages: Discovering the New Map of Men's Lives*. Ballantine Books, 1999.

Shulman, Diana. *Co-parenting after Divorce: How to Raise Happy, Healthy Children in Two-Home Families*. Winnspeed Press, 1996.

Summers, Nancy. *The Silver Lining: The Unexpected Advantage of Divorced Women*. Vinyard Publications, 1992.

Teyber, Edward. *Helping Children Cope with Divorce*. John Wiley & Sons, 2001.

Turecki, Stanley, M.D. *The Difficult Child*. Bantam Books, 2000.

Weiner-Davis, Michelle. *Divorce Busting: A Revolutionary and Rapid Program for Staying Together*. Fireside, 1993.

Wetzler, Scott, Ph.D. *Living with the Passive-Aggressive Man: Coping with Personality Syndrome of Hidden Aggression—From the Bedroom to the Boardroom*. Fireside, 1993.

Worthen, Tom, Ph.D. *Broken Hearts . . . Healing: Young Poets Speak Out on Divorce*. Poet Tree Press, 2001.

Recommended Support Groups

DivorceCare (*www.divorcecare.com*) is comprised of thousands of groups meeting throughout the United States, Canada, and 20 other countries. While DivorceCare groups are sponsored by various churches, the groups are nondenominational and open to all.

Beginning Experience (*www.beginningexperience.com*) is an international support program for divorced, separated, and widowed individuals and their families intended to facilitate the resolution of the grief surrounding the breakup of a marriage/relationship and to promote healing.

The Mars Venus Workshops (*www.marsvenusinstitute.com*) are interactive classes based on the books by Dr. John Gray. Gray's instructors facilitate the workshops, which are located around the globe.

Couple Communication Programs (*www.couplecommunication.com*) teach partners interpersonal skills for effective talking, listening, conflict resolution, and anger management. Workshops are available in many countries.

Marriage Enrichment, Inc. (*www.gbgm-umc.org/me-incOH/main.asp*) is a nondenominational, not-for-profit, nationwide Christian organization sponsoring the Marriage Enrichment workshops developed by Dr. Carl T. Clarke, a clinical psychologist and former pastor.

Retrouvaille (*www.retrouvaille.org*) is a program offering the chance for husbands and wives to rediscover themselves and each other as they work toward healing and renewing their marriage.

Marriage Encounter (*www.wwme.org*) provides weekend experiences as well as continuing support activities that present practical, ongoing communication tools for couples seeking to strengthen their marriage. Available in many countries.

Al-Anon and Al-Ateen (*www.al-anon-alateen.org*) are programs offering support for the spouse or child of an alcoholic. The website gives information and references to local groups.

Recommended Hotlines

National Domestic Violence Hotline: (800) 799-SAFE (7233). Staffed 24 hours a day by trained counselors providing crisis assistance, shelter information, and legal advocacy. Toll-free number for hearing-impaired: (800) 787-3224.

RAIN Hotline (Rape, Abuse, Incest National Network): (800) 656-HOPE (4673). Toll-free number to locate rape crisis centers throughout the United States. Also available as a domestic violence shelter if no other support is available.

Further Bibliography

This section includes books, articles, interviews, and transcripts mentioned in the text or used as references, but not listed above.

ABC News Good Morning America. "Linda Waite and Pepper Schwartz debate over controversial study about divorce." Burrelle's Information Services. July 11, 2002.

ABC World News Now. "Forgiveness." January 3, 2001.

Anderson, Julia. "On the job friendship can help women." *The Columbian* (Vancouver, WA). April 21, 2002.

"Anxiety, alcoholism, affairs: they're often evidence of men's middle-aged 'metapause.' " *People*, August 15, 1980.

Apter, Terri and Ruthellen Josselson. *Best Friends: The Pleasures and Perils of Girls' and Women's Friendships*. Crown Publishers, 1998.

Bortz II, Walter, M.D. *Dare to Be 100*. Fireside Books, 1980.

Bowlby, John. *Attachment and Loss, Vol. 1. Attachment*. Basic Books, 1969.

Brody, Steve, Ph.D. and Cathy Brody, M.S. *Renew Your Marriage at Midlife*. G. P. Putnam's & Sons, 1999.

Brookoff, D., K. K. O'Brien, C. S. Cook, T. D. Thompson, and C. Williams. "Characteristics of participants in domestic violence: Assessment at the scene of domestic assault." *JAMA*, 1997.

Carruthers, Malcolm, M.D. *Maximising Manhood: Beating the Male Menopause*. HarperCollins, 1996.

Chew, Peter. *The Inner World of the Middle-Aged Man*. Macmillan Publishing Company, 1976.

Courtenay, Will H. "Behavioral factors associated with male disease, injury, and death: evidence and implications for prevention." *The Journal of Men's Studies*, September 22, 2000.

Dott, Andrew B., M.D. and Caroline Dott, MSW, Ph.D. *www.midlife-passages.com/depressi.htm*.

Epperly, Ted D. and Kevin E. Moore. "Health issues in men: Part II. Common psychosocial disorders." *American Family Physician*, 2000: 62.

Erikson, Erik H. *Childhood and Society*. W. W. Norton & Company, 1963 edition.

———. *The Life Cycle Completed*. W. W. Norton & Company, 1982.

———. *Youth and Crisis*. W. W. Norton & Company, 1969.

Farrell, Michael P. and Stanley D. Rosenberg. *Men at Midlife*. Auburn House Publishing Co., 1981.

"Fast cars, fast women, faster divorces." *The Gold Coast Bulletin*, August 11, 2001.

Fisher, Helen E. *Anatomy of Love: The Natural History of Monogamy, Adultery, and Divorce*. W. W. Norton & Company, 1992.

Golan, Naomi. *The Perilous Bridge: Helping Clients through Mid-Life Transitions*. The Free Press, 1986.

Gordon, Barbara. *Jennifer Fever: Older Men, Younger Women*. Harper & Row, 1988.

Gordon, J. S. and S. Curtin. *Comprehensive Cancer Care: Integrating Alternative, Complementary, and Conventional Therapies*. Perseus Publishing, 2000.

Gratch, Alon, Ph.D. *If Men Could Talk . . . Here's What They'd Say*. Little, Brown & Company, 2001.

Griffin, Victoria. *The Mistress: Histories, Myths and Interpretations of the "Other Woman."* Bloomsbury, 1999.

Hallberg, Edmond Co. *The Gray Itch: The Male Metapause Syndrome*. Stein & Day, 1978.

Health News Network. "Hans Selye's general adaptation syndrome." *www.healthnewsnet.com/gap.html*.

Heisel, William Knight. "When medications hinder your sex life, take action." *The Orange County Register*, April 4, 2001.

Hill, Dr. Aubrey M. *Viropause/Andropause: The Male Menopause*. New Horizons Press, 1993.

Humphreys, Andrew. "Pfizer turns drugs into highly successful brands." *Med Ad News*, No. 3, Vol. 21.

Hunter, Ski and Martin Sundel. *Midlife Myths: Issues, Findings, and Practice Implications*. Sage Publications, 1989.

Jung, C. G. *The Basic Writings of C.G. Jung*, trans. by R.F.C. Hull, Princeton University Press, 1990.

Karen, Robert. *The Forgiving Self: The Road from Resentment to Connection*. Doubleday, 2001.

Keyes, Ralph. *Chancing It: Why We Take Risks*. Little, Brown & Company, 1985.

Kruger, Arnold. "The mid-life transition: crisis or chimera?" *Psychological Reports*, 1994: 75.

Kuczynski, Alex. "Good times and bum times, but she's here." *The New York Times*, September 29, 2002.

Levinson, Daniel J. (with Charlotte N. Narrow, Edward B. Klein, Maria H. Levinson, and Braxton McKee). *The Seasons of a Man's Life*. Ballantine Books, 1978.

Lim, Justin K. *Male Mid-Life Crisis: Psychological Dynamics, Theological Issues, and Pastoral Interventions*. University Press of America, 2000.

Madden, Robin, M.D. Ph.D. Interview. October 16, 2002.

McMillan, Len D. *An Owner's Guide to Male Midlife Crisis: Midstream without a Paddle*. Pacific Press Publishing Association, 1986.

McNamara, Mary. "Are we raging out of control?" *Los Angeles Times*, August 6, 2000.

Nolan, William A., M.D. *Crisis Time! Love, Marriage and the Male at Midlife*. Dodd, Mead, & Company, 1984.

NYO Staff. "Asian students battle bigotry." *New York Observer*, July 16, 2001.

Peterson, Karen S. "Unhappily wed? Put off getting that divorce." *USA Today*, July 11, 2002.

Quintanilla, Michael. "Beauty and the beast: male grooming is growing up. Think masks, scrubs and (dare we say it?) makeup." *Los Angeles Times*, September 9, 2001.

Raffel, Lee. *Should I Stay or Go? How Controlled Separation Can Save Your Marriage*. Contemporary Books, 1999.

Rhodes, Dr. Sonya. *Second Honeymoon: A Pioneering Guide for Reviving the Mid-life Marriage*. William Morrow & Company, 1992.

Russell, Cheryl. "The baby boom turns 50." *American Demographics*, December, 1995.

Safer, Jeanne. *Forgiving and Not Forgiving: A New Approach to Resolving Intimate Betrayal*. Avon Books, 1999.

Sanford, John A. and George Lough, Ph.D. *What Men Are Like: The Psychology of Men for Men and the Women Who Live with Them*. Paulist Press, 1988.

Schwartz, Pepper. *Everything You Know about Love & Sex Is Wrong: Twenty-five Relationship Myths Redefined to Achieve Happiness and Fulfillment in Your Intimate Life*. Putnam, 2000.

Sevrens, Julie. "Men slow to seek heath care may sacrifice years." *News & Record* (Greensboro, NC). September 30, 1997.

Shek, D.T.L. "Mid-life crisis in Chinese men and women." *Journal of Psychology*, 1996: 130.

Spiegel, D., J. R. Bloom, and H. C. Kraemer, et al. "Effect of psychosocial treatment on survival of patients with metastatic breast cancer." *Lancet*, 1989: 2.

Steffens, Sara and Fran Metcalf. "Heartbreak sex." *Courier Mail*, October 13, 2001.

Tavris, Carol. *Anger: The Misunderstood Emotion*. Simon & Schuster, 1989.

Tennov, Dorothy. *Love and Limerance: The Experience of Being in Love*. Stein & Day, 1980.

U.S. Census Bureau, 2000.

Wallerstein, Judith S., Julia M. Lewis, and Sandra Blakeslee. *The Unexpected Legacy of Divorce: The 25 Year Landmark Study*. Hyperion, 2001.

Walters, Peter. "Dalai Lama's words simple, powerful, enlightening." *Confederated Umatilla Journal*, June 30, 2001.

Warrington, Hannah. "Bayer, Glaxo's impotence drug delayed in U.S. market." *Bloomberg News*, July 24, 2002.

"Where's Momma?" *Human Behavior*, November, 1973.

www.aboutimpotencetherapies.com.

www.cop.ufl.edu/safezone/doty/dotyhome/wellness/HolRah.htm. "Social Readjustment Rating Scale developed by Holmes and Rahe."

www.healthnewsnet.com/gap.html.

www.midlife-passages.com/depressi.htm.

INDEX